THE MARKET RESEARCH TOOLBOX

THE MARKET RESEARCH TOOLBOX

A Concise Guide for Beginners

Edward F. McQuarrie

SAGE Publications
International Educational and Professional Publisher
Thousand Oaks   London   New Delhi

For information address:

SAGE Publications, Inc.
2455 Teller Road
Thousand Oaks, California 91320
E-mail: order@sagepub.com

SAGE Publications Ltd.
6 Bonhill Street
London EC2A 4PU
United Kingdom

SAGE Publications India Pvt. Ltd.
M-32 Market
Greater Kailash I
New Delhi 110 048 India

Printed in the United States of America

Library of Congress Cataloging-in-Publication Data

McQuarrie, Edward F.
The market research toolbox: A concise guide for beginners /
author, Edward F. McQuarrie.
p.   cm.
Includes bibliographical references and index.
ISBN 0-8039-5856-0 (acid-free paper). — ISBN 0-8039-5857-9 (pbk.:
acid-free paper).
1. Marketing research—Methodology.   I. Title.
HF5415.2.M383   1996
658.8'3—dc20   95-41753

This book is printed on acid-free paper.

96 97 98 99   10 9 8 7 6 5 4 3 2 1

Sage Production Editor: Tricia K. Bennett
Sage Typesetter: Christina M. Hill

Contents

PART II

PART III

Preface

Market research refers to any effort to gather information about markets or customers. Market research is more necessary today than ever before because of the increased complexity of the modern economy. At the level of specific industries or firms, the general rule is that whenever uncertainty increases, the need for market research becomes more acute. That is, whenever markets grow or change complexion, economic conditions fluctuate, competition intensifies, or technology evolves rapidly, the payoff from doing effective market research can be substantial.

Of late, the kinds of firms who have invested heavily in market research and the kinds of people who get involved in market research have changed dramatically. Twenty years ago, mainstream, packaged-goods companies were the major practitioners of market research, and the number of people who directly participated in market research was limited. Internal to the firm, the market research department was charged with hiring and supervising outside consultants on a project-by-project basis. These consulting firms in turn employed technical specialists for things such as questionnaire design and statistical analysis. The firm's marketing managers, in consultation with market research staff, set the basic parameters for the research study before it was put out to bid. Finally, executives set overall budgets and chose whether to heed the results of the research. And that was that. Research and development (R&D) engineers did not materially participate except to receive the final report. The *quality* function had scarcely been invented.

Today, a much wider range of businesses feel the need to conduct market research, including manufacturers of high-technology products and providers of financial services. Similarly, a much more diverse group of employees has become involved in the design and conduct of market research. This is partly because some of the newer techniques cannot be delegated to specialists and mostly because the contemporary business environment demands that *everyone* in the firm be customer and market focused. Three types of nonmarketing participants are worthy of special note: (a) engineers, including the design and development engineers who create new products, the manufacturing engineers who install and maintain production processes, and the technical services engineers and application specialists who do postsales work with customers; (b) quality professionals whose responsibilities now extend far beyond inspecting products for defects toward the achievement of total customer satisfaction; and (c) industrial designers, human interface specialists, and others who focus on the interaction between product and user. In most firms, these people do not have a standard marketing or even business education. Nonetheless, the pressures of business require that they grasp the basic procedures for learning about customers and markets. Such learning has become a crucial part of their job responsibilities.

In light of the growing interest in and need for market research, this book was written to fill a gap. Although hundreds of books on market research have been published, most follow one of two models: (a) thick tomes surveying the whole of market research and intended for use as textbooks in university classrooms and (b) thin volumes, covering one technique only, often at an advanced level, and aimed at an audience of specialists. What did not exist at the time of writing was a *thin* volume intended to provide an *overview* to the interested reader seeking a place to *begin*. The assumption underlying this book is that you need either to get your bearings (What is conjoint analysis anyway?), to conduct some market research (Would a focus group make sense here?), or to interpret a market research effort that someone else has championed (Can this survey help me?).

In a second departure, this book is written primarily for *managers*. Business students who seek a management career also will benefit, but in tone, manner, and approach, the envisioned audience is a manager who has to decide whether to do market research, what kind of research to do, and what objectives to pursue. Although it should prove useful as supplemental reading in a variety of courses, this book is not a textbook. It does not conform to university pacing, style, tone, or degree of abstraction. Instead, the treatment strives to be concrete and specific: Do this. Don't do that. Watch out for this problem. Try this solution. The guiding image is that managers are impatient people subject to conflicting demands who must act now. This book offers a practical approach addressed to their needs.

A third departure is a focus on business-to-business and technology examples. Modern market research as we know it was pioneered in the 1930s, 1940s, and 1950s to meet the needs of companies such as Procter & Gamble, Quaker Oats, and Ralston Purina. Soap, cereal, pet food, and the like continue to be prominent among the examples and illustrations used to teach market research in the typical university course. This is entirely appropriate for textbooks aimed at a broad audience because consumer packaged-goods companies continue to spend large sums on market research and to provide many of the career opportunities in market research. However, living in California's Silicon Valley, my experience base is different. The research problems with which I am familiar preoccupy companies such as Hewlett-Packard, Apple Computer, and Sun Microsystems. Markets are small and concentrated, products are complex and expensive, customer expenditures are driven by the need to solve real business problems, and technologies are dynamic and rapidly changing. Although much of the accumulated wisdom of market research is just as relevant to Hewlett-Packard as to Procter & Gamble, it has to be taught differently. The audience I have in mind is impatient with examples based on the marketing of detergent to housewives. This target audience does not want to have to make the translation from mass markets, simple products, and stable technologies to their own rather different situation.

If you fall within the core audience for this book, you are a beginner and not a specialist. One of the important contributions of the book is to direct you to further reading. There exists an enormous amount of specialized material on market research. Part of my job is to help you sort through it so that you can find the next book that you need to read. If you intend to actually execute a particular market research project yourself, you certainly will need to read more than this book—for the sake of brevity, this book will not go into a great deal of depth on any single technique but will merely open the toolbox and explain its contents and application. This book *will* tell you what a hammer is, what it does to a nail, when it is useful to drive nails, and when you might be better off to use a bolt and wrench. It will not train you to do carpentry. The assumption throughout is that "carpenters" (experts) are available to you. Thus, the focus can be on the background context and the questions that need to be asked *before* you hire a carpenter (or embark on your self-taught career as a carpenter).

Plan of the Book

Part I describes how to think about market research in the context of business decisions. Market research is only a means to the end of business success. It aids in but can never guarantee the achievement of profit. Market research almost always costs money—hard, assignable dollars that come out of an individual manager's budget. Therefore, as with any investment, market research has to be justified by its expected return. Part I answers questions about what market research is, what kinds of market research techniques exist, what objectives can be met by market research, and what payoff to expect from market research. The purpose of Part I is to equip you with the necessary vocabulary and organizing concepts to think intelligently about how market research might assist you in your own situation.

Part II of the book describes six traditional market research techniques: secondary research, customer visits, focus groups, surveys, choice modeling, and experimentation. I call them traditional techniques because, for the most part, the rationale and implementation were initially worked out 30, 40, or 50 years ago. These are the techniques that generally come to mind in business circles when one mentions market research. Each technique is discussed using a standard format: how it works, who does what when, what it costs, examples or applications, cautionary notes, tips for success, and further reading.

Part III begins by describing nontraditional techniques of market research that have evolved in recent years to meet the needs of business-to-business marketers in general and technology firms in particular. It concludes with a chapter on how five common business applications (e.g., segmenting a market or developing a new product) might be addressed through combining several individual research techniques into a research strategy. This section addresses the issue of how multiple techniques can be joined and sequenced for maximum advantage.

Who Should Read This Book

R&D Project Managers. You have the responsibility to make something happen, with the development of a new product being the clearest example. It is your job to marshall people and resources to achieve a project goal. Today, that includes doing market research. Although you can reasonably expect considerable assistance from marketing staff, the effectiveness of the market research done for you will often be a crucial determinant of the project's success; consequently, there is a limit to how much you can delegate in this area. You probably will be among the most intent and focused readers of this book inasmuch as when you finish you will have to *act*—to request a budget, spend money, or commit employee time. This book tries to answer as many of your questions as possible.

Program Managers. Your responsibilities are similar in many respects to those of the project manager, with one crucial exception: Your output is seldom anything so tangible as a new product. Most of what you do consists of enhancing, improving, supplementing, or supporting your firm's central products or services (or maintaining and averting any decline in the quality of those products or services). In consequence, the budgets you directly control are typically minimal (if any even exist). You will be particularly interested in those parts of this book that describe low-cost and no-cost approaches to gathering information on markets and customers.

Product Managers—Marketing. You probably do have a business education, perhaps an MBA, with one or more market research courses under
your belt. For you, this book serves two purposes: It provides a refresher
course, reinforcing your grasp of basic principles now that your schooling
lies years in the past, and it is something you can give to members of your
work group to bring them up to speed on the contribution of market
research generally and the rationale for individual research techniques. If
you are in a business-to-business or technology firm, you also may find
this book helpful in linking your business education, which probably
emphasized packaged-goods examples, to your current job.

Engineers. You are curious about the market research techniques you
hear mentioned. You are probably also a little skeptical whether market
research is of any use in your particular situation, in which technical
innovation is key. This book will help you to make informed decisions
about whether to embark on or accept the results of particular market
research efforts.

Quality Professionals. Your charge today is customer satisfaction, not
defect minimization. Depending on the culture of your firm, you may have
assumed responsibilities classically assigned to the marketing function—
that is, building a commitment to customer satisfaction on the part of
employees throughout the firm. You have a solid statistical training but
have grown uneasy about the heavy reliance on surveys commonly found
within the quality literature. This book helps you to grasp the possibilities
inherent in the whole toolbox. It also will help you to think about statistics
in the context of social science—that is, the behavior of humans—rather
than the production context in which your statistical education began.

Executives. You are at a level where business strategy is set. As with
many contemporary executives, you probably are receptive to the idea that
being market focused is important, but also, it is not entirely clear to you
how this laudable goal can be implemented in a timely and cost-effective
manner. For you, this book serves two purposes. It provides a briefing and
reminder of what market research can and cannot do (this is particularly
helpful if your background is technical and not business based), and it
provides a resource that you can recommend to your people and to the
training function within your firm.

Instructors. You probably do *not* teach the marketing research course. The course you *do* teach (industrial marketing, new product development, marketing strategy, competitive analysis, etc.) includes a project or other activities in which students must gather data or make recommendations about data gathering. You often have wished there was a book you could assign as supplemental reading that would help students think about data gathering (including where to find additional information on specific research techniques). Until this book, you faced the unpalatable alternatives of (a) expecting them to find on their own a comprehensive market research textbook and read the appropriate sections (in that you cannot assume that your students have necessarily taken the market research course); (b) hoping they will find, assemble, and read specialist volumes on focus groups, surveys, and so forth and then make an intelligent choice among them; or (c) scheduling enough office hours to help students work through the above issues.

Students. You need an overview of market research that can be quickly grasped, a set of tips and cautions to help you through your initial efforts, and advice on where to go to learn more.

EDWARD F. MCQUARRIE

Acknowledgments

I received all of my training in market research in the field, and I would like to acknowledge some of the individuals and firms from whom I learned the most. Particular thanks go to Nick Calo, Mike Kuhn, Ron Tatham, and many others at Burke Marketing Research, where I got my start moderating focus groups and doing copy tests of advertisements; to Dave Stewart of the University of Southern California and Bill Bon-Durant, formerly of Hewlett-Packard's Market Research & Information Center, for introducing me to best practices in the planning of market research (Chapter 2 builds directly on material developed by them and taught at HP for many years); to Lew Jamison and Karen Thomas, now or formerly at Sun Microsystems, for inviting me to design a course on market research, giving me the confidence to attempt this book; to my editor Marquita Flemming at Sage, for actually giving me the impetus; to

Nancy Gordon, Klaus Hoffmann, and Tomas Lang, of HP Marketing Education, for the initial opportunity to teach marketing research to managers and for helpful encouragement; to Shelby McIntyre of Santa Clara University, for many insights into effective market research; to Al Bruno and Sharmila Chatterjee, now or formerly of Santa Clara University, for insightful comments on the manuscript; to my clients at Amdahl, Apple Computer, Cadence Design, CIGNA, Compaq, Fluke, Harris, Hewlett-Packard, Motorola, Sun Microsystems, Varian Associates, and elsewhere, for challenging questions concerning the application of market research to specific business situations; and to Karen Graul, Marketing Department secretary at Santa Clara University, for typing so many drafts so well.

PART I

1

Nature of Market Research

Market research is a *marketing* activity, and marketing is a philosophy concerning how to succeed in business. As a philosophy, marketing competes against other philosophies that make different prescriptions for business success. Notable among competitors to the marketing philosophy are the *innovation* philosophy (success comes from technology leadership), the *quality* philosophy (success comes from building the highest quality products), and the *financial* philosophy (success comes from making the most efficient use of resources). As a philosophy, marketing argues for the primary importance of focusing on markets and customers as guides to business strategy. From this perspective, market research consists of anything and everything the firm does to learn about and understand markets and customers. Adherents to the marketing philosophy are distinguished by their willingness to grant

3

Figure 1.1. Reciprocal Relationship of Business Strategy and Market Research

prime authority to market facts and customer needs when choosing among courses of action. Practitioners of other philosophies do not so much ignore markets and customers as relegate them to a secondary role, as two among many checkpoints, to be consulted toward the end rather than the beginning of decision making.

Business strategy is the plan of action a firm develops to achieve its goals. Business strategy and market research have a reciprocal relationship as shown in Figure 1.1. Sometimes market research comes *after* business strategy. That is, (a) a plan is hatched in the minds of management and (b) market research is conducted to determine the odds of success with respect to each alternative approach to implementing the plan (and what can be done to improve these odds). Alternatively, sometimes market research comes *before* business strategy. At a time of transition, management may choose first to embark on an intensive examination of markets and customers and second to formulate new strategies. Most of the time in successful firms there is an ongoing dynamic relationship between business strategy and market research. Ideas are conceived and then refined through specific market research projects, while at the same time ongoing market research yields new ideas for gaining strategic advantage. Firms that are relatively more market oriented will place proportionately greater influence on the *strategy discovery* function of market research, whereas firms that are relatively less market oriented will tend to emphasize the *strategy confirmation* function.

These two ideas—that there is a reciprocal relationship between strategy and market research and that market research can be used for purposes of either discovery or confirmation—help to clarify several questions that typically bedevil engineers and other technically trained professionals when they approach the question of whether to do marketing research.

Technological Innovation and Market Research

In some engineering circles, market research is regarded with suspicion as an inherently conservative activity with a built-in bias against anything really new. If you have engaged in this dialogue, as I have on numerous occasions, you know that this accusation will almost always be followed by a telling anecdote intended to clinch the argument. The birth of Apple Computer is a favorite example: We know that Steve Jobs and Steve Wozniak did no formal market research whatsoever prior to launching the product that kicked off the enormous personal computer market. Furthermore, it is somewhat hilarious to imagine an innocent citizen in 1977 receiving an evening phone call from a market researcher who asks a series of questions along the lines of the following: "Do you need a computer at home for your personal use? What would be the most important application for this computer? How large a memory should it have?" With a glint in his eye, our sparring partner will fold his arms and conclude, "There! If the founders of Apple Computer had done market research, the Apple II would never have been introduced, they'd be millions of dollars poorer, and a very useful tool would have seen its diffusion into society woefully retarded."

Many anecdotes similar to the story of Apple Computer are readily available. You may even encounter a particularly sophisticated debater who will attempt a one-two punch by bringing in the devastating failure (at least initially) that attended the introduction of New Coke in 1984. New Coke provides the converse story: We know that millions of dollars *were* spent on market research, and we know that Coca-Cola is among the most successful companies in the world, indicating that that market research was probably ably conducted. Nonetheless, this intensive market research effort still could not prevent an embarrassing failure.

These anecdotes would appear to confirm two truths: (a) that business success can occur without market research and (b) that the presence of market research does not guarantee business success. From here, our debating partner wants to jump to the next conclusion: "Therefore, market research is generally a waste of time for technology companies." For further support, our debating partner will point to the rapid pace of change in technology, the inability of customers to envision or even articulate how they would use something that does not yet exist, together with the sheer complexity of technological products, as explanations for why market research is ineffectual when technological innovation is the goal.

Of course, anecdotes are not really very effective tools of argument. You come up with a success story in which market research was not done, and I respond with a different anecdote in which market research played a crucial role. Neither of us persuades the other. What this debate needs is good research consisting of a large number of cases that would allow us to estimate the relative frequency of instances in which market research proved crucial to success versus the relative frequency of cases in which it proved superfluous. In fact, such research has been conducted and accumulated for more than 20 years (see the Suggested Reading section). The results are unambiguous: When one steps back from individual war stories to the aggregate level and examines large numbers of innovations or compares large numbers of successful versus failed new products, one finds that a majority of the success stories are characterized by disciplined efforts to understand customers and markets, whereas a majority of the failures exhibit a neglect of or incompetence in market research.

Those are the facts. On average, successful new product development efforts do more market research, do it better, and do it earlier, whereas on average, failed new products exhibit the reverse profile. These facts accommodate any anecdote our sparring partner may produce. Because the claim is only that market research is useful *on average,* we can readily acknowledge instances in which market research does no good or fails to prevent harm. Apple Computer and New Coke were not the first and will not be the last such examples. Ultimately, it comes down to a question of odds: Do you want to gamble that your company, your technology, and your project are among the exceptions in which market research happens to be a waste of time? I would suggest that your stockholders would very much prefer that you play the percentages and direct your energies to the question of what specific kind of market research would do you the most good in your particular situation, not to a misguided effort to succeed while remaining innocent of any kind of market research.

To lay the foundation for answering the question of what kind of market research to do and when to do it, this chapter and the next lay out some basic frameworks. The remainder of this chapter classifies tools—shows you the compartments of the toolbox, if you will. The next chapter locates each tool within the building project, showing which tools provide a foundation, which provide the superstructure, and which provide the finishing details.

Distinction 1:
Exploratory Versus Confirmatory Research

The goal of exploratory market research is *discovery*. The underlying questions are, What is new? and What are we missing? The goal of confirmatory techniques is *resolution:* Is this the right choice? What specific results can we expect? You conduct exploratory market research to open your eyes and broaden your vision. You conduct confirmatory research to narrow your options and concentrate your efforts along the optimal path.

Exploratory techniques tend to coincide with information needs early in the decision cycle, whereas confirmatory techniques make sense later on. *Decision cycle* refers to the set of decisions made over the course of a project. *Projects* would include, for example, the development of a new product, an investigation of whether a market should be segmented into submarkets, an inquiry into whether to concentrate on a particular niche, or a study of customer satisfaction.

The distinction between exploratory and confirmatory techniques is absolutely crucial. As will be explained when we discuss the individual techniques, all the factors that make a market research technique useful in an exploratory context tend to render it highly suspect in a confirmatory context. Stories are legion of the misuse of exploratory techniques (i.e., the focus group) to obtain a degree of certainty that can be achieved only by more expensive and arduous means. It is equally a mistake to use confirmatory techniques when discovery is the goal. Where the misuse of exploratory techniques can lead to serious mistakes, the misuse of confirmation techniques is more analogous to incurring opportunity costs as opposed to out-of-pocket costs. When confirmatory techniques are misapplied, discoveries fail to occur, opportunities go unrecognized, and insight is not achieved. Hasty use of confirmatory techniques at too early a point in the decision cycle incurs the risk of getting wonderfully precise answers to the wrong questions.

Distinction 2:
Marketing Intelligence Versus Research Studies

Market research studies involve efforts sharply bounded in space and time and expressly linked to some project such as development of a new product. These studies have a clear beginning and end, and their cost is assigned to an individual project budget. Virtually all of the techniques whose names are common knowledge among businesspeople—the questionnaire, the focus group, the experiment—are applied as part of market research studies. Marketing intelligence, by contrast, is an ongoing activity not tied solely to a specific project. As the root metaphor suggests, marketing intelligence consists of bits and pieces of information gained from agents in the field, from diverse publications, and from having your ear to the ground and is extensively sifted by expert judgment.

For market intelligence gathering, the core competence required for success is one part database management and one part organizational leadership. It takes vision for a firm's management to commit resources to the gathering of market intelligence not tied directly to any specific project budget. A minimally adequate effort would involve maintaining a library in which reports bought by subscription from consultants such as the Gartner Group, DataQuest, or IDC are filed. Leading firms (Hewlett-Packard and Sun Microsystems are two examples) have begun to put these resources on-line so that they can be accessed at the individual manager's desktop. Still to come are database systems that will combine published reports with the firm's own reports of past market research studies and with more diverse kinds of intelligence, such as trip reports from customer visits. Only now are free-form text databases (e.g., Lotus Notes) developing to the point at which masses of amorphous marketing intelligence can be collated, searched, and sifted. Great strides in this area can be expected over the next decade.

For market research studies, the core competence is problem formulation skills. Most business situations do not present themselves as clearly delineated problems but as tangled messes that might be approached in a variety of ways. As will be developed in the next chapter, to succeed in a market research study requires that the sponsoring manager clearly articulates the decision to be addressed and the specific kinds of information needed. Most of the other skills needed to complete a market research study (i.e., expertise in sample selection, experimental design, and statistical analysis) can be purchased from outside vendors. But the correct formulation of the research question ultimately resides with the sponsoring manager. Although good consultants can assist in formulating problems, the authority to determine the real underlying problem rests with the manager who has profit-loss responsibility for the product or service.

It is useful to distinguish between relatively exploratory and relatively confirmatory forms of *both* market intelligence gathering and market research studies. The following are examples of each:

Market intelligence, exploratory. Once a month you log onto a database such as Dialog and perform a keyword search for every mention in any article of each of your three largest competitors. These articles are reviewed for possible insights into competitive strategy.

Market intelligence, confirmatory. You subscribe to a service that monitors sales in or shipments to some particular distribution channel. Results are periodically analyzed in terms of sales trends for the channel, changes in market share for yourself and competitors, and so forth.

Market research, exploratory. You conduct focus groups to get a better grasp of how your brand is regarded, relative to key competitors, in a certain market segment.

Market research, confirmatory. You conduct a survey of 1,000 customers to assess perceptions of your brand relative to the competition on each of eight significant performance attributes.

As shown by these examples, market intelligence efforts generally yield a range of conclusions or provide data that can be analyzed in a variety of different ways or will be relevant to multiple projects or decisions. The theme again is that a considerable amount of human judgment has to be supplied to derive the expected benefits from the data collection. Of course, judgment also is required to get the best results from market research studies, but much of that judgment gets exercised up front in the design of the research study. Market intelligence allows for more opportunistic analyses, whereas analysis of market research studies is more constrained by the initial design.

All of the four examples just given focus on issues of competitive standing. Of course, this is far from the only possible focus for market intelligence and market research. Broadly speaking, market intelligence and market research studies can be focused on either *markets* or *customers*. Customers are individual human beings with feelings, perceptions, opinions, and reactions—customers make decisions. Markets are aggregates consisting of human beings, institutions, resource flows, and environmental forces and contexts. Markets grow or shrink in size, concentrate or fragment, become more competitive or less so, and change quickly or slowly. Research on customers rests on the discipline of psychology, whereas research on markets relies on the discipline of economics. To give some sense of the difference in emphasis, here are four more examples, all of which concentrate on customers rather than on competition (competition is an aspect of markets). Some customer examples include the following:

Market intelligence, exploratory. Whenever a customer visit occurs, the person making the visit always asks the customer, "If you could change any one thing about this product, what would that be?" Answers are logged in a text database and reviewed quarterly.

Market intelligence, confirmatory. You subscribe to a survey that periodically measures buying intentions for your product and others.

Market research, exploratory. You conduct 24 customer visits to identify problems and needs that should be addressed when you design the next generation of an existing instrument product.

Market research, confirmatory. You conduct an experiment to determine which of three pricing levels provides the optimum combination of market share and profit margin for a new instrument product.

Financial Justification for Market Research

Thus far I have argued that you probably have to do some kind of market research and that the real questions are what kind to do and how much to

Exhibit 1.1 Setting Limits on the Market Research Budget

Formula

Budget = $K \times R \times F$

where

K = The cost of being wrong—how much lower gross profit will be if you make a mistake in product design, choice of target market, and so on.

R = Percentage reduction in the likelihood of making such a mistake, if you were to conduct effective market research

F = The feasibility percentage set by corporate or business unit policy. Where $K \times R$ indicates the *maximum* market research budget—the point at which the cost of doing market research would exactly equal its benefits—F deflates this amount to determine the feasible budget—the actual spending target.

Example

Suppose that the new product under consideration is expected to produce sales revenue of $60 million and a gross profit of $15 million. Suppose also that a mistake in design such that the product fails to address a significant customer need will reduce that $15 million profit to zero, that effective market research might reduce the likelihood of making such a mistake by 10%, and that the feasibility percentage for this firm has been set at 5%.

Then,

Market research budget = $15,000,000 × .10 × .05 = $75,000

---

do. The key distinctions have clarified the kinds of marketing research that exist. The second question (How much?) boils down to a financial analysis of the expected payback of various levels of investment in market research. Exhibit 1.1 presents a rule of thumb for determining the maximum feasible expenditure on market research that a given project can justify (the minimum expenditure, of course, is zero).

The first step is to estimate K, the cost of being wrong in this project. For instance, if on introduction, crucial features in the product are lacking, what would that cost you? If you end up targeting the wrong application or the wrong group of customers, how expensive would this mistake be? In thinking about "cost," it is best to focus on gross profit (or loss) and not on revenue. Gross profit equals sales revenue minus cost of goods sold and is calculated before overhead is taken into account. Gross profit is the appropriate level of analysis because it takes more than a dollar of revenue to cancel out a dollar of market research expenditure, because only the profit portion of the revenue dollar counts. Also, in large firms, overhead is often not under the control of marketing managers, who are in any case measured on their gross profit performance. In a venture capital or small-firm situation, of course, one might conduct the analysis directly in terms of shareholder profit—the ultimate goal. Market research is an out-of-pocket cost and the goal is a return—a profit—on this expenditure, the same as on any other expenditure incurred to produce the new product.

The second step is to estimate R, the percentage reduction in the probability of error that could be achieved by conducting an effective market research effort. This number is going to be quite a bit more fuzzy than the first number, but the principle is clear: How much help could good market research offer in a situation of this kind? Note that when the situation is terminally confusing or when it is already quite clear, then R will be very small. In fact, R will be large only when candidates for the "right" decision can at least be glimpsed *and* when there are a manageable number of such candidates *and* when there is little confidence or consensus among decision makers about which candidate decision is the best one to make.

The third step in the analysis is to set the *feasible* market research expenditure as a fraction of the maximum expenditure. This fraction will typically be relatively small for all kinds of good reasons, including most notably the amount of guesswork involved in determining the maximum budget and also the requirement that market research actually yield a profit and not just cover its cost. Because there generally exists more direct levers on profit than market research (speeding up product development is always a logical alternative use for the dollars in the case of most technology firms), my intuition is that the feasible percentage (F) should typically run between 5% and 20% of the maximum budget (see Exhibit 1.1). This is another way of saying that your estimated return on investment (ROI) for your market research budget should fall in the range of 500% to 2000%. This again reflects the relative remoteness of market research as a factor in the final determination of profit, in addition to many other things having to go right before a profit can be achieved. Even here, financially savvy project managers always will ask themselves whether there might be another use for some or all of these funds that would promise an even higher return. On a final note, one of the market research responsibilities of marketing executives at the vice president level ought to be to determine what a customary, usual, and reasonable feasibility percentage would look like for their line of business and to enforce this percentage across projects so that it becomes a reliable guide for initial project planning. In the absence of such a policy, it is very difficult for an individual project manager to argue for a particular feasible percentage.

The utility of Exhibit 1.1 becomes apparent when it is combined with basic cost information concerning market research. This cost data will be discussed in more detail under the individual techniques, but some basic guidelines can be given. First, at the time of this writing, $10,000 was about the floor for any execution of a particular market research technique (market intelligence can, of course, cost much less, and we will return to this point). A more common level of expenditure for an individual technique would be $20,000 to $30,000, and most projects of any magnitude will want to combine multiple research techniques. As a rule of thumb, then, a meaningful market research effort over the life of, say, a new product development project would cost in the $50,000 to $100,000 range.

With this cost information in hand, we can put the equation in Exhibit 1.1 to work. First, let the corporate gross profit margin be 25%, let the reduction in error attributable to good market research be 10%, and let the feasible budget percentage be 5%. With these numbers, we see that the new product must have revenue potential of about $60 million if one is to justify a market research budget on the order of $75,000. Specifically, the following is required:

1. Assuming that making an important mistake in product design will cause the product only to break even rather than making a normal profit, the cost of a mistake is $15 million (25% gross profit × $60 million in sales revenue).
2. Applying the equation in Exhibit 1.1, the maximum market research budget is then $1.5 million (due to the expected 10% reduction in the odds of making a mistake).
3. Applying the feasibility percentage of 5% yields the budget of $75,000.

By jiggering any of the assumptions just made, we easily can get the required revenue potential down to $20 million or so. Thus, software and other technology businesses exist with gross margins well above 25% and even 50%. Alternatively, it may be more reasonable to assume that a mistaken product will produce an actual *loss* rather than breaking even. Moreover, the situation might be such that the reduction in error due to good market research will be more than 10%. Finally, a more market-focused corporate culture might set a higher feasibility percentage than 5%. By a somewhat more heroic rearrangement of our assumptions (combining any two of the revisions just named), we could get the revenue level down to around $10 million. To get it any lower, we would have to start skimping on the market research effort; even then, $5 million is probably the lower limit for expected sales revenue impact if we are to justify a sophisticated market research effort including at least two distinct data collection efforts and costing several tens of thousands of dollars.

Quite a number of useful conclusions emerge from this financial analysis. On the one hand, any Fortune 1000 corporation has many, many products with annual revenue potential in the tens of millions of dollars range, indicating again the pervasive opportunity for conducting market research. On the other hand, most small businesses and most technology start-ups will have to use ingenuity and rely heavily on intelligence gathering rather than on research studies per se. Continuing along these lines, the *higher* the profit margin, the *greater* the opportunity to do market research (or make any other investment in long-term market success). Conversely, the *lower* the capital costs for introducing and then terminating a failed new product, the *less* the justifiable expenditure on market research. When I began consulting for insurance and financial services firms, I was quite struck by the contrast between their research budgeting and that of the equipment manufacturers with whom I was most familiar. To design and manufacture a new instrument or other electronic product inevitably entails a substantial research and development (R&D) and capital expenditure. To introduce a new financial service or program will often incur modest costs that are several orders of magnitude less. In such cases, actual market introduction provides a relatively quick and inexpensive test of whether the program was or was not a good idea; consequently, up-front market research has to be inexpensive if it is to be done at all. The moral of the story: If it will not cost you much to be wrong, you should not spend very much on market research.

The logic of the equation in Exhibit 1.1 has particularly troubling implications for *program managers*. This job category includes people who manage documentation, customer service, or lines of product accessories and the like. Program managers have no less need for market and customer information than project and product managers (these are parallel job titles in the engineering and marketing functions), but their efforts seldom have the kind of assignable revenue impact required to justify a substantial market research budget. Two solutions make sense for people in the program manager position. The first is to concentrate on intelligence gathering, and the second is to find ways to piggyback on the market research efforts of project and product managers. If a program manager can add a question or two to a research study, this may have little effect on the cost of the study but yield an invaluable supplement to the ongoing intelligence effort. Program managers who regularly execute such piggyback strategies gain a constant stream of research data at little direct cost.

On a final note, a more subtle implication of the financial equation in Exhibit 1.1 is that a short-term focus makes it difficult to adequately budget for market research. For technology companies in particular, substantial market research efforts may be best focused at the *product platform* level and not at the level of an individual product configuration. That is, just as home stereo manufacturers offer a variety of amplifier power and quality levels, so also many technology products come in large and small, high-end and low-end versions, each aimed at a particular application or industry segment. Although each is a somewhat different product, all rest on the same basic assembly of technologies—the platform. Sales at the platform level, especially over the several years of life of the platform, will almost always be large enough to justify a substantial research budget (moreover, whereas product life cycles have often shrunk to months, platform life cycles still last for years). Unfortunately, accounting systems and organizational groupings often are structured in terms of products. If the platform has no budget code and if no team or individual has platform responsibility, then effective budgeting for market research becomes difficult.

Stepping back, Exhibit 1.1 provides a way of acting on the truism that market research has to be considered as an investment. It becomes clear that market research really *is* expensive and that the stakes have to be high for its justification. Conversely, the exhibit serves as a lever for use with those penny-wise and pound-foolish technical managers who choke at the idea of spending $50,000 on something as intangible and squishy as market research. When a new product line is expected to generate revenue on the order of $100 million and there are some excruciating uncertainties concerning its design and intended audience, then a market research expenditure of $100,000 is a trivial price to pay to improve the odds of success. Note again that this kind of high-stakes situation is most likely to arise at the level of a product line or product platform and is much less common at the level of an individual product configuration or stock-keeping unit.

Note also that whereas the *K* component in Exhibit 1.1 provides a bracing reminder that market research planning is basically about money, the *R* component provides an equally important reminder that market research itself really boils down to uncertainty reduction. To the extent that you feel certain about what will happen or what will work, then market research grows less necessary. For instance, if management has already made up its mind (for good or bad reasons), then market research cannot reduce the odds of a wrong decision because it is not going to have *any* effect on the decision. Studies conducted under these circumstances are just politics and basically a waste of time. Conversely, when uncertainty is very high—your environment is essentially chaotic—market research may be besides the point. Inasmuch as this situation is the more common one in technology firms, an example might help. Suppose that the success or failure of a given project hinges entirely on whether the technical standard to which it adheres does or does not end up dominating the market some years hence. Suppose further that the dominance or defeat of that technical standard is not within the control of company management or of any definable group of people—that it will, in fact, be a function of so many interlocking factors that it is impossible to grasp them all or depict their interrelations. In this situation, the most that market research may be able to offer is an early warning of whether the technical standard is or is not moving toward dominance. If that early warning would not be helpful, then it may be best to spend nothing at all on market research in this connection and put the money to other uses, such as lobbying for the chosen standard at technical gatherings.

Perhaps you expected more than "uncertainty reduction" from market research. You hoped, in a nutshell, to achieve some kind of *guarantee* of making the right decision. Not to be too blunt, but you are naive. Market research is a social science, not a physical science, and a young social science at that. It can reduce uncertainty but never eliminate it. On average, across a large business, over a period of years, this small reduction in uncertainty can be very lucrative and repay the cost of the research many times over. But all market research can ever do is reduce the odds of making a costly error and increase the odds of making a profitable decision. If instead it is certainty that you want, then I suggest you go to a chapel.

Suggested Reading

Barabba, V. P., & Zaltman, G. (1991). *Hearing the voice of the market.* Cambridge, MA: Harvard Business School Press.

> This work emphasizes marketing intelligence and how to institutionalize, within the corporate organization, best practices in the use of market information.

Bennett, P. D. (1995). *Dictionary of marketing terms* (2nd ed.). Chicago: American Marketing Association.

> This is helpful if you encounter an unfamiliar term in a discussion of research methods.

Bonnet, D. C. L. (1986). Nature of the R&D/marketing cooperation in the design of technologically advanced new industrial products. *R & D Management, 16,* 117-126.

Utterback, J. M. (1974). Innovation and the diffusion of technology. *Science, 183,* 620-626.

> Utterback is the classic source on technology-push versus demand-pull paths to successful innovation. Bonnet reviews subsequent studies yielding similar results.

Cooper, R. G. (1993). *Winning at new products: Accelerating the process from idea to launch.* Cambridge, MA: Addison-Wesley.

> Cooper provides a review of studies of new product success and failure and discusses best practices at each stage of development.

Day, G. S. (1994). The capabilities of market driven organizations. *Journal of Marketing, 58,* 37-52.

> Day integrates current thinking about where market research fits among other marketing capabilities. This is a good guide to the literature on market orientation and its contribution to profitability.

Dickinson, J. (1990). *The bibliography of marketing research methods.* Lexington, MA: Lexington Books.

> This is a good place to start when you want more detailed information on some particular topic (e.g., use of response incentives in survey research) or technique (e.g., multidimensional scaling).

Slywotsky, A. J., & Shapiro, B. P. (1993). Leveraging to beat the odds: The new marketing mind-set. *Harvard Business Review, 71,* 97-107.

> Slywotsky and Shapiro show how the investment approach applied to marketing research in this chapter can be applied more generally within a broader context of marketing strategy.

The following publications provide a means of keeping up with developments in market research:

> *Journal of Advertising Research (JAR)* emphasizes research on all aspects of advertising, has a strong practitioner focus, and often reports studies based on real-world data.

> *Journal of Marketing (JM)* does not publish articles on market research per se, but each issue contains a literature review that briefly abstracts recent articles on a variety of topics, including market research.

> *Journal of Marketing Research (JMR)* is the leading academic journal in this area. Highly technical articles emphasize tests of theories and new analytic techniques.

> *Journal of the Marketing Research Society (JMRS)* is a leading British journal and has historically been strong in the area of qualitative research.

> *Journal of Product Innovation Management (JPIM)* is the best source for current thinking on new product development. In addition to original research, each issue abstracts and reviews books and articles in this area.

> *Marketing News (MN)* is the newsletter of the American Marketing Association and regularly publishes guides to market research software, focus group facilities, and so forth. In May or June of each year, a review of the largest 50 market research vendors gives phone numbers and a profile of services offered.

> *Marketing Research: A Magazine of Management and Application (MR/MOMA)* is addressed to practitioners and provides many detailed examples of the actual market research practices and policies of leading firms.

> *Marketing Science (MS)* is a prestigious academic journal that emphasizes the development and testing of mathematical models of marketing phenomena such as price elasticity and effects of various budget levels.

Planning for Market Research

It is easy to describe what not to do in preparing for market research. The following are three cautions that can save you a great deal of grief:

Do not fund market research in a reactive mode.
Do not fixate on a favorite market research tool.
Do not assume that one tool or one research study will be enough.

Implicit in these cautions is the notion that market research needs can be anticipated and planned for when the budget for a project is drawn up. Also implicit is the idea that every market research tool is specialized and has limited applicability. In this regard, imagine if you encountered a homeowner who claimed that he had built his entire house using nothing but a nine-inch socket wrench—you would be more appalled than amazed. Why would anyone go through all those contortions when there is an entire toolbox available that has evolved expressly to make house construction as efficient as possible? Yet it is not uncommon to encounter businesses that, faced with a need for market research, *only* conduct surveys or *only* do customer visits or *always* do focus groups. You will be much more effective if you can acquire a sense of the distinctive contribution of each tool together with an understanding of how the tools work together over the course of a project.

Figure 2.1 breaks down the decision cycle associated with any project into four steps. Again, as examples of projects you might keep in mind enterprises such as the development of a new product, the development of a new ad campaign, or expansion into a new market.

The first step is to *scan the environment.* What is going on? What is out there? This activity of environmental scanning can be thought of as a sharpening and focusing of the activity of intelligence gathering, which, as argued earlier, should be ceaseless. Thus, Figure 2.1 shows the first stage in the cycle as emerging from the plane of intelligence gathering. An example of scanning the environment would be to compile analysts' reports on the strategies, strengths, and weaknesses of your major competitors. In this early stage, you would probably also examine reports on how the market is segmented, who the biggest users of this product category are, what applications dominate, and so forth.

The second step in the decision cycle is to *generate options.* What are the possibilities? What specific directions might be worth pursuing? What choices do we face? For example, if a product line has come to seem aged and tired, there probably is more than one possible approach to rejuvenating it, and all of these need to be identified and explored. If you are seeking to expand your market, you will want to identify all the possible groups that could be targeted for expansion. Likewise, before selecting a new theme for your ad campaign, you would want to examine a variety of candidates. Stage 2 can be thought of as the creative part of the decision cycle. The goal is to broaden your horizons so that you do not neglect opportunities or miss possibilities.

The third step in the cycle is to critically examine and then *select an option* from among those generated in Stage 2. Which of these options is best? How much will this option achieve for us? It is at this stage that you must decide exactly what functionality a product will offer. This is where

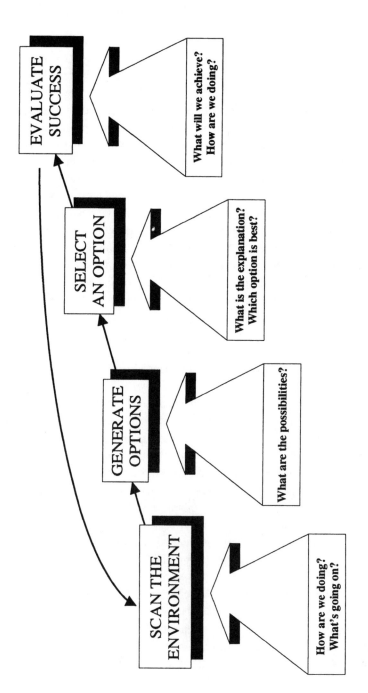

Figure 2.1.

21

you determine which one among several markets is likely to be the largest, the most lucrative, or the best protected against competitive counter-attack. Stage 3 is crucial because resources are always limited. This is a uniquely stressful stage because you have to commit to one option and abandon the remainder. You may have generated half a dozen attractive candidates for market expansion, but lack of money, people, or time will force you to select one or a few on which to concentrate your efforts.

The fourth and final step is to *evaluate the success* of the decisions you made. How well did we do? Did we take market share away from the competitor we targeted? Did the new ad campaign change attitudes among the intended audience? How satisfied are customers who bought the new product? Results from the fourth stage are added to the stock of market intelligence possessed by the firm. These results also influence management's ongoing strategic review of business directions. Recalling Figure 1.1 and the reciprocal influence between strategy and market research, Figure 2.1 depicts the entire decision cycle as occurring within the context of ongoing strategic review. In business, decisions never stop.

Matching Tools to Decisions

The purpose of this model of the decision cycle is to help you decide which market research tools might be useful at any given point. To do this requires a third concept that can bridge the gap between decision stages on the one hand and the toolbox on the other. Here the concept of a *research objective* is helpful. A research objective states, in a single sentence, what result you hope to achieve through the use of some particular research technique. An example might be, "Identify areas of satisfaction and dissatisfaction with our current product offering." Good research objectives always start with an action verb. If you leave out the verb, you end up with something vague and empty—a wish, hope, or yearning.

Articulating your objective in this concise and concrete way has two benefits. First, it forces you to stop and think: Really, what is it that I want to accomplish? This is a nontrivial benefit. Most managers are buffeted by numerous conflicting deadlines, interruptions, sudden changes of course, and the like. A requirement to spell out the goal for this market research expenditure usefully concentrates the mind.

TABLE 2.1 Examples of Research Objectives

Verb	Some Possible Objects
Identify	Problems, opportunities, choice criteria
Define	Concept, design, potential
Describe	Decision process, usage, work environment
Explore	Perceptions, reactions, remedies
Generate	Hypotheses, alternatives, explanations
Evaluate	Feasibility, attractiveness, potential
Select	Product, concept, ad execution
Test	Preference, direction, profitability
Measure	Growth, size, frequency
Prioritize	Segments, needs, opportunities
Monitor	Trends, competition, events
Track	Spending, satisfaction, awareness

A second benefit of spelling out your objective is that often you will discover that the objective you have just written out is insufficient—it reflects only part of what you are trying to accomplish. To continue the example given earlier, you may well realize that your actual objective is more comprehensive and better corresponds to the following two-part statement: (a) Identify areas of satisfaction and dissatisfaction, and (b) prioritize areas of dissatisfaction according to degree of negative impact on revenue. Now that you have reached this point, it may strike you that the research procedures required to *identify* areas of dissatisfaction may not be the same as those required to *prioritize* them. To identify requires an exploratory approach that can uncover what exists; to prioritize re- quires a precise and confirmatory approach that can take a set of existing things and order them from best to worst or most to least. With that realization, you are well on your way to articulating a research strategy encompassing multiple data collection activities that holds some promise of meeting all your information needs.

Table 2.1 lists a dozen verbs that often form the basis of research objectives, along with some examples of typical objects for each verb. For instance, one can *identify* opportunities or problems or choice criteria or *select* markets or product concepts or ad themes. Table 2.1 may not reflect *all* the verbs that provide a useful starting point for formulating market research objectives, but it should cover most situations you will encounter. If you want to use a verb from outside this list, ask yourself whether it

TABLE 2.2 Decision Stages, Research Objectives, and Research Tools

		Tools	
Stage	*Objectives*	*Primary*	*Supporting*
Scan environment What's out there? What's going on?	Identify, describe, monitor	Secondary research, customer visits	Focus groups, surveys
Generate options What are the possibilities?	Generate, define, explore	Customer visits, focus groups	Secondary research
Select an option How much will we achieve? Which one is best?	Evaluate, test, select, prioritize	Experiments, sur- veys, choice models, usability tests	Secondary research
Evaluate success How well did we do?	Measure, track	Surveys, secondary research	Customer visits

really adds anything and especially whether it is concrete and specific enough. For instance, in my experience, a favorite word of businesspeople in the context of market research is *validate*. But what does this mean? To validate is to confirm the correctness of some idea we hold—in other words, to test. Whereas validate is a long and somewhat unfamiliar word, thus vague in applicability and diffuse in meaning, *test* makes it clear that we are going to attempt to prove the truth of some proposition using fairly rigorous means. With validate, we could kid ourselves that a dozen customer visits might be enough to validate our ideas, whereas with test we are unlikely to convince ourselves or anyone else that a dozen interviews is adequate. Hence, test is a more useful word because it gives more guidance as to what kind of market research might be able to fulfill our objective. Validate blurs the focus of your work; test sharpens it.

Table 2.2 maps decision stages and individual research techniques onto research objectives. For each stage, certain research objectives are characteristic and customary. In turn, each research tool plays a primary role in achieving certain objectives and can contribute secondarily to the achievement of others. Table 2.2 is intended to serve several purposes.

First, it provides the means to perform a quick check on a research proposal submitted by someone else in your organization. If someone says they want to do focus groups to select which ad execution will have the strongest appeal, a warning light should go off in your mind. Focus groups are not listed among the tools used to select an option. Second, Table 2.2 provides a planning and scheduling tool for specifying needed market research over the life of a project. It affords you multiple opportunities to ask questions such as, What activities am I going to undertake so as to scan the environment? or How will I go about identifying possible new applications for this instrument? A third benefit of Table 2.2 is that it provides three possible entry points to kick off your market research planning. Sometimes you will feel most confident about where you are in the decision cycle, sometimes a particular verb such as *identify* or *explore* will be the hook, and sometimes you will be focused on a particular research tool. You can enter Table 2.2 from any of these points and build toward a complete research strategy from that point.

Table 2.3 provides an alternative viewpoint on the relationships mapped in Table 2.2. Here the individual research tools provide the rows and the individual research objectives the columns in a matrix. Whereas Table 2.2 was decision focused, Table 2.3 is tool focused. It facilitates the correct use of each tool via the graphic symbols, which specify that the tool is a primary means of achieving an objective (double check mark), contributes secondarily to that objective (single check mark), or is generally misleading or dangerous in the context of a certain objective (*X*-mark). Blank cells indicate either that a tool bears little relationship to a certain objective— hence, no warning is needed—or else that it is meaningless to make any overall endorsement or prohibition because so much depends on how the objective is interpreted in the specific case.

Effective Application of Research Tools

Parts II and III of this book will go into considerable detail about the strengths and weaknesses and best applications and misapplications of individual research tools. It is possible, however, to introduce briefly each tool here and to simultaneously walk the reader through Tables 2.2 and 2.3. The focus here is on the research objectives and how each tool relates

TABLE 2.3 Research Tools Matched to Research Objectives

| | Stages and Objectives | | | | | | | | | | | |
| | Scan Environment → | | | Generate Options → | | | → | Select an Option | | | → Evaluate Success | |
Tool	Identify	Describe	Monitor	Generate	Define	Explore	Test	Evaluate	Prioritize	Select	Measure	Track
Secondary research	✓✓	✓✓	✓✓	✓	✓	✓	✓	✓	✓	✓	✓✓	✓✓
Customer visits	✓✓	✓✓	✓✓	✓✓	✓✓	✓✓	X	X	✓	X	X	
Focus groups	✓	✓		✓✓	✓✓	✓✓	X	X	✓	X	X	
Survey research	✓	✓✓	✓	X	✓	X	✓✓	✓✓	✓✓	✓✓	✓✓	✓✓
Choice models	X					X	✓✓	✓✓	✓✓	✓✓		
Experiments	X	X		X	X	X	✓✓	✓✓	✓✓	✓✓	✓✓	✓

to them, whereas subsequent chapters will focus on the tools themselves. The detailed justification for the summary judgments rendered in the discussion that follows will be deferred until the chapters on individual tools.

SECONDARY MARKET RESEARCH

This research technique encompasses any data collected by someone else for some other purpose, which also happens to be useful to you. Secondary research can be composed of internal or external data. Common examples of external secondary research include data compiled by the U.S. Bureau of the Census and other government agencies, reports written by consulting firms and sold to interested parties (e.g., "Five-Year Sales Projections for Color Laser Printers"), and publicly available information, such as articles in the trade press. Common examples of internal secondary research include sales records, customer databases, and past market research reports.

Secondary research has obvious relevance to the environmental scanning stage of the decision cycle. It will almost always be quicker and cheaper to answer a question through secondary data than through conducting your own primary market research. In virtually every project, your first step should be to amass whatever secondary research is available and glean whatever insights you can. Secondary research can be used to identify market opportunities, describe market structure, and monitor competitive activity. For example, suppose you install, maintain, and service videocameras used for security purposes. Using secondary research, you might discover that automated teller machines (ATMs) in nonbank locations offer a rapidly growing market for video security. You might encounter this fact in the trade press or perhaps in a syndicated report on market trends for small videocameras.

Because secondary research is composed of so many diverse activities, one or another kind of secondary research also may play a supporting role in both generating *and* selecting options. Thus, a market opportunity identified at an earlier point may be defined further through secondary research. Continuing with our example, secondary research might help you formulate two market expansion options to (a) target large banks with extensive off-premises ATM networks or (b) concentrate on convenience store chains that recently have installed ATMs in their stores. Information on market size or market structure gained through secondary research also may help you evaluate the relative profitability of two different strategic options. Thus, your own internal records may indicate to you that cameras mounted in very small stores require on average more servicing than cameras located in larger buildings. This might be sufficient to cause you to select convenience stores as your initial target market, inasmuch as cameras associated with their new ATMs are likely to generate substantial service revenue.

A particular type of secondary research becomes of primary importance when you reach the fourth stage. Quite often you will want to evaluate the outcome of a decision by measuring changes in market share for yourself and key competitors. Syndicated reports (regular studies, produced by independent consulting firms, to which you and other members of your industry subscribe) are often a source of market share data. Alternatively, your own review of secondary data may help you answer this question. Thus, if you can find information on how many ATMs were installed in a region last year, you can compute your share of these installations relative to your goals.

CUSTOMER VISITS

In a program of customer visits, a dozen or more customers are inter-viewed at their place of business. Customer visits can be thought of as a combination of field research with interviews. Customer visits, along with several other tools, are of primary importance in the environmental scanning stage. Listening to customers describe problems can help to identify new product opportunities. Walking around the customer site facilitates rich descriptions of product applications. Regular contact with customers helps you to monitor emerging market trends and changes in the business environment.

Customer visits are also crucially important, along with focus groups, in the generation of options. This is because the loosely structured nature of these interviews allows for surprises. Similarly, extensive exposure to customers and their way of viewing the world often provides a fresh perspective. Moreover, the intensive dialogue that a 2-hour, face-to-face interview permits helps you to define issues and explore perceptions in depth.

Customer visits should never be used to test, evaluate, or select options. The small sample size, the convenience nature of the sample (i.e., not random), and an unknown degree of interviewer bias makes it impossible to trust the results of customer visits in this connection. (As will be developed subsequently, these same shortcomings are of much less moment when customer visits are used appropriately to scan the environment and generate options.) The lone exception is when you are planning to visit *all* your customers. This might be possible because these customers are all other divisions internal to your firm or because the market for your product is very limited with only a few large buyers. If you can visit all your customers, then you have a census and not a sample, and the limitations cited earlier are less pressing. Even here, the portion of your visit devoted to testing and selecting among options probably will have a quite different feel relative to the rest of the visit and relative to more conventional applications of the visit tool. As stated earlier, to explore and to confirm are two very different activities.

Customer visits may sometimes play a minor supporting role in the evaluation of decision outcomes. Although in principle, customer visits are just as ill-suited to measuring and tracking as to testing and selecting, visits can potentially supplement more formal and confirmatory approaches, such as survey research. Although it is important to know whether your customer satisfaction numbers have gone up or down, it will not always be clear *why* the pattern of results takes the form it does. In this situation, a series of visits to both customers whose satisfaction has increased and to customers whose satisfaction has not changed or has gotten worse often will be illuminating. This is really another way of saying that the final stage of one decision cycle tends to merge with the first stage of the next.

FOCUS GROUPS

In a focus group, 8 to 12 people meet in a special facility for approximately 2 hours. The facility allows for you to view the group from behind a one-way mirror and to make audio- and videotapes. The group discussion is moderated by a professional interviewer in accordance with objectives set by you. Focus groups are very similar to customer visits in their profile of suitable and unsuitable objectives but somewhat more narrow in their applicability. The broader applicability of customer visits stems from its field research aspect (you go to the customer site) and the amount of time spent with individual customers.

Focus groups are simply a particular kind of interview, and this makes them useful in the initial exploratory stages of the decision cycle in which you are scanning the environment and generating options. For instance, you might do some focus groups to identify emerging issues as viewed by customers within a particular segment of the market. At a later point, you might use focus groups to explore the pros and cons of several possible themes being considered for a new ad campaign. Part of generating options is defining these options in as much detail as possible, and the give-and-take of group interaction can be quite productive in this respect.

Focus groups are probably more effective at exploring, defining, and generating (Stage 2) than at identifying, describing, and monitoring (Stage 1)—hence, their relegation to a contributing role during the environmental scanning stage. The power of focus groups comes from the interaction of customers within the group and whatever synergy results. The stimulus of group interaction is particularly useful when the goal is to generate fresh perspectives, define the difference between subgroups within the market, or explore consumer reactions. It is less useful when you want to cast a wide net or get the lay of the land.

As with customer visits, focus groups should never be used to select among options. The problem again centers on the small, bad samples of customers involved. Similarly, the skill brought by the outside interviewer to the conduct of focus groups is more than outweighed by the distorting potential of group influence and dominant participants. Problems of group influence and conformity pressure and the condition that focus groups are a laboratory rather than field procedure make it impossible to recommend their use for even a contributing role during Stage 4, evaluation of outcomes. In short, focus groups constitute a more specialized tool than either secondary research or customer visits.

SURVEY RESEARCH

A survey takes place when a fixed set of questions is asked of a sample of customers. The sample usually will be large and in many cases will be carefully selected to represent the total population of customers. The comments to follow assume a telephone survey executed with a reasonably large and carefully selected sample in which the questions are largely *descriptive.* (Some implementations of two other techniques described next—choice modeling and controlled experiments—also will make use of a questionnaire, but the nature and structure of the questions will be very different and not focused on description per se.)

Surveys can play a supporting role in environmental scanning. If you need a fairly exact factual description of the behaviors and simple perceptions of some customer group and if such data cannot be gleaned from existing secondary research, then it may make sense to execute a survey. If, however, good secondary data already exist, it will rarely be cost-effective to do your own survey, unless this takes the form of a small, fast, tailored survey directed at filling in a few gaps in the available secondary data. If the needed secondary data do not exist and if you simply must have precise descriptive data on matters such as the frequency of certain applications among particular customer groups, the average dollar amount of equipment purchases, or the average rating of your speed of response relative to key competitors, then a survey may make sense.

You should ask yourself, however, whether you really need precise descriptive data at this early point in the decision cycle. Is it really that important to be able to state with precision that 54% of the time, this medical instrument will be used on auto accident victims, 24% on mothers undergoing childbirth, 18% on victims of gunshot wounds, and 4% with others? At this early point, what is the value added by these precise percentages as opposed to what you could gain from a program of customer visits? A couple of dozen visits would probably reveal that auto accidents, childbirth, and gunshot wounds were "major" applications, even though the exact percentages would be unknown. In addition and in contrast to the limited data supplied by a survey, the visits would provide opportunities to describe in depth how each of these applications place different demands on the instrument and on hospital staff, how this instrument interfaces with other equipment in the hospital, and so forth. Such rich descriptive data often will be more useful early in the decision cycle than the thinner but more precise data yielded by surveys.

It is even more important to understand that surveys are far less useful in the generation of options than customer visits or focus groups. The relative weakness of surveys at this point in the decision cycle has several sources: (a) that the questions to be asked are fixed in advance, (b) the reality that the implementers of the survey (the people on the phone) probably lack the ability, the motivation, or the opportunity to deeply probe customer answers, and (c) the unfortunate truth that the impersonal nature of the survey contact (the certain knowledge that one's responses are but grist for the statistical mill) will inhibit and limit the customer's investment of the energy required for discovery, exploration, and depth. Surveys are a confirmatory tool whose proper purpose is to limit, narrow, and specify; hence, this tool is largely incapable of expanding, broadening, and reconfiguring your understanding. Go easy on surveys early in the decision cycle.

Survey research comes into its own at the third stage of the decision cycle. All of the features that had been of dubious relevance or even liabilities at the earlier stages are here either neutralized or converted into strengths. In Stage 3, the time for discovery and in-depth insight is past; now it is time to make hard choices and allocate limited resources. Perhaps you have only the resources to write new software for one or at most two of your instrument's applications, and you must determine which application predominates. Large investments may follow from decisions of this type, and it makes sense to invest a good sum of money in determining precisely which application is largest, is growing the fastest, or has the weakest competitive presence.

Survey research also will be of primary importance in the evaluation of outcomes. The classic example is the customer satisfaction surveys now conducted by many firms. These are usually telephone surveys, often conducted by a neutral outside firm, in which a standard series of questions is asked, focusing on product and vendor performance. The surveys often are repeated on a quarterly basis so that changes in satisfaction can be tracked over time. Another example is the tracking studies conducted after initiating an advertising campaign. These telephone surveys track awareness, brand attitude, and perceptions in those areas addressed by the advertising campaign. Here again, descriptive precision is an absolute requirement, else comparison over time becomes impossible.

CHOICE MODELS

There are at least two major approaches in use, one of which takes the form of a questionnaire, whereas the other consists of cards or other stimuli that contain different permutations of product attributes (i.e., conjoint analysis). Regardless of format, the goal of all choice modeling procedures is to build a model of how a customer makes a choice among the various product offerings available in a market. The goal of choice models is thus to answer questions such as, Which product attributes drive the purchase decision?

Choice modeling is a valuable tool with strictly limited applicability. It makes little sense to use choice models during environmental scanning. Too little is known to justify use of a precise and narrowly focused tool of this kind. Choice models are not really appropriate for the generation of options either. This is because to perform choice modeling one must be able to say exactly what the key product attributes are, and part of the purpose of generating options is precisely to discover what product attributes might matter at all. Logically, environmental scanning and options generation precede and lay a foundation for more confirmatory techniques such as choice modeling.

The primary purpose of choice models is to assist in the selection of the best option, in the specific sense of the optimal product configuration. When serious uncertainty remains about whether one bundle of features or another is the most attractive to consumers or about how to construct the optimal bundle of features, choice models may provide the answer. By the time one gets to the fourth and final stage of evaluating outcomes, the time for choice models has passed.

EXPERIMENTS

In the simplest form of an experiment, you would administer two different treatments to two equivalent groups of customers and measure the response of each group to the treatment. The purpose of an experiment is to test which among a small number of treatments stimulates the greatest response. For example, you may be considering two different headlines for use in a direct mail pitch for some product or service and you want to know which version will be most successful.

Similar to choice modeling, experiments are a narrowly applicable but extremely valuable tool. They are *not* of much use in the initial stages of environmental scanning and option generation or in the final stage of outcome evaluation. Early in the decision cycle you do not know enough to design a good experiment, whereas toward the end of the cycle you want market data, not experimental data. Rather, experiments also are primarily intended for use in option selection. In fact, their design corresponds exactly to the structure of many business decisions: that is, which of these options is the best? Moreover, experiments can sometimes answer one additional question that is generally not within the purview of choice models: How much will we achieve? For instance, the response rate for the winning headline in the direct mail example would allow us to estimate what the response rate will be for the mass mailing, and this in turn allows us to draw up a pro forma income statement showing the cost of the promotion and the anticipated revenue gain.

Summary

Now that the contents of the market research toolbox have been spread out before you and each tool has been briefly introduced and situated within the decision cycle, a few summary statements are in order.

1. Secondary research is *the* all-purpose market research tool. Partly because of the great diversity of the types of information that can be gained and partly because much secondary research is both cheap and quickly obtainable, your first impulse in planning any inquiry into customers and markets should be to ask, Has somebody else already gathered the information I need? It is simple common sense: Do not reinvent the wheel.

2. Customer visits and surveys are the most heavily used forms of primary research. The application of both these tools is a matter of asking questions and getting answers. If the issues with which you are concerned can be phrased as direct questions that customers are able to answer, then customer visits or surveys probably will be rewarding.

   Customer visits anchor the exploratory end of the continuum. Here you may know what your question is or what some of your questions may be but have no certainty about what kinds of answers are even possible. By contrast, surveys anchor the confirmatory end. Here, you know both the key questions and the range of possible answers, and your goal is to pin down the exact frequency of each possible answer.

3. The selection of options, unlike the other decision stages, requires highly specialized research tools. As discussed earlier, several tools are used only here. It is an error and a mark of ignorance if the management of a firm exclusively conducts customer visits, surveys, or a review of secondary resources when the primary goal is to select an option. Selecting the best option—pricing is a good example—often requires you to go beyond asking questions of customers and instead to create environments in which customers act or choose so that you can analyze these behaviors to infer the answers you require.

Dos and Don'ts

Do plan on using a variety of techniques over the course of a project. Make every effort to find the right tool for the job at hand. Every tool is specialized, and no tool is perfect.

Don't confuse exploratory and confirmatory techniques. Do not try to squeeze precision out of tools that cannot provide it, and do not expect discoveries and new insights out of tools whose purpose is to narrow down the possibilities and eliminate options.

Don't fixate on specific research tools. Keep the focus on the decision to be made and on what information would be most helpful. Let the tool follow from the research objective.

Suggested Reading

Blankenship, A. B., & Breen, G. E. (1993). *State of the art marketing research.* Lincolnwood, IL: NTC Business Books.

> A managerially focused textbook, the authors' extensive experience as practitioners shows in the detailed examples of how market research is applied to formulate and test business strategies.

Blattberg, R. C., Glazer, R., & Little, J. D. C. (1994). *The marketing information revolution.* Boston: Harvard Business School Press.

> These authors offer a wealth of ideas for how information technology can be used to enhance the collection of marketing intelligence. This supplements the more sociological and behavioral approach of the Barabba and Zaltman book given as suggested reading in Chapter 1.

Churchill, G. A. (1995). *Marketing research: Methodological foundations* (6th ed.). Chicago: Dryden.

> This is a good example of a standard textbook on marketing research. It gives more detailed coverage of the specific tools discussed here and a more thorough introduction to the statistical analysis of market research data.

Davis, R. E. (1993). From experience: The role of market research in the development of new consumer products. *Journal of Product Innovation Management, 10,* 309-317.

> A veteran consumer goods marketer (30 years at Procter & Gamble) summarizes the role of market research over the development cycle.

PART II

3

Secondary Research

Secondary market research refers to any data gathered for one purpose and by one party and then put to a second use by or made to serve the purpose of a second party. Secondary market research is thus the broadest and most diffuse tool within the toolbox, in that it includes virtually any information that can be reused within a market research context. Secondary research is also the closest thing to an all-purpose market research tool, in that virtually every project will make some use of secondary data and almost any decision stage may incorporate some kind of secondary research. As a general rule, relatively speaking, secondary research also will be the cheapest and quickest form of market research. You ignore or skimp on it at your peril. Its range of application is limited only by your ingenuity.

It is helpful to distinguish between internal and external secondary research. Internal secondary data consist of information gathered elsewhere within your firm. The major categories include (a) sales reports, (b) customer databases, and (c) reports from past primary market research. Sales reports generally give data broken down by product category, region, and time period. More sophisticated systems also will give breakdowns by distribution channel, level of price discount, customer type (large, medium, small), and similar categories. Customer databases might include (a) a recording of brief descriptive data on all accounts (industry, contact person, phone number, purchase history) or a log of tech support or response center calls or (b) a record of inquiries in response to advertisements and the like. Records of past primary market research will include results of surveys and focus groups conducted in prior years, accumulated customer visit trip reports, and so forth.

External secondary research includes (a) information gathered by government agencies such as the U.S. Bureau of the Census, (b) information compiled for sale by commercial vendors, and (c) various kinds of public and quasi-public information available from diverse sources. Government agencies collect an enormous amount of demographic (e.g., the Bureau of the Census) and economic trend data (e.g., Federal and State Departments of Commerce). In recent years, the U.S. government also has done more to help companies seeking to export by providing information on overseas markets. Entire volumes are devoted to simply listing and cross-referencing various government reports.

An important kind of secondary data available from commercial vendors is known as the syndicated report. For a syndicated report, an analyst will compile a variety of data, using libraries, databases, phone calls, and even some primary market research, such as interviews or surveys, to address a topic such as "Trends in the color printer market 1995-1998." The goal is to sell the report to as many printer-related companies as can be persuaded to buy. Syndicated reports may be one-time efforts or may appear periodically. Because the appetite for data is so huge, especially in technology markets, a whole industry of syndicated report vendors has grown up to satisfy this appetite. These commercial vendors function as one part librarian, one part statistician, one part detective, and one part proxy market researcher. They employ analysts who are in the business of being industry experts, and a certain number of hours of these analysts' time can be purchased along with the vendor's reports.

Public and quasi-public data sources include anything published in a magazine or newspaper. Most industries have a few magazines devoted to coverage of companies, events, and trends. A few industries, such as the computer and the telecommunications industries, are the focus of a slew of publications. Similarly, most industries of note will, on occasion, be the subject of a feature article in the *Wall Street Journal, New York Times, Los Angeles Times,* or other respected newspapers. Moreover, trade associations, university survey research centers, nonprofit agencies, and others will all publish data from time to time. With the spread of computerized information retrieval services (everything from the traditional Dialog to the Worldwide Web on the Internet), it has become easier to bring together data from a wide range of sources and publications.

Procedure

Three types of procedure are relevant here:

1. Steps to be taken at the firm level, to facilitate the collection and use of secondary research throughout the firm
2. Steps to be taken by individuals within a firm in connection with a *market research project*
3. Steps to be taken by individuals within a firm as part of *ongoing market intelligence* efforts

The logic of the first distinction is that an individual contributor or manager will find it difficult to do excellent secondary research unless an infrastructure has already been put in place at the firm level. The logic of the second and third distinctions is based on the difference between a market research study and ongoing market intelligence gathering, as set out in the first chapter, and the differing demands these place on secondary research.

STEPS TO BE TAKEN BY THE FIRM

Upgrade the Corporate Library. Although major corporations have had internal libraries for many years, of late the demands on and the potential benefits from these libraries have rapidly escalated. Today, in the marketing area, the primary holding is not books or even periodicals but the syndicated reports bought from various vendors. Because so many individuals will have a use for particular reports on occasion, most corporations of any size centralize the purchase of market research reports and have the collection maintained by either a division of the library or a department within the market research area.

A carefully thought-out strategy of which reports to buy from which vendors is a must. It may be quite difficult for an individual project manager to get the funds or find the time to locate a valuable report that is not part of the collection—if he or she even learns of its existence at all. Consequently, the best way to promote the use of secondary data is to arrange to have on hand most of the most useful reports.

A good library will have an effective indexing and cataloguing strategy so that relevant data can be located easily. A good library also will be on the lookout for specialized resources—services that compile statistics, bulletins that bring together articles from a variety of trade publications, and so forth. Finally, a good library will keep up with new technology for collecting and distributing information. Note in this regard that by 1994, large market research vendors had begun to distribute their reports on CD-ROM and that by 1995, a number of vendors, including Dow Jones, Knight Ridder, and Ziff-Davis Interchange, had begun to provide personal electronic clipping services, wherein a semi-intelligent agent searches for articles meeting a profile set up by a user. Phrases such as "the information society" and "the data explosion" are not hype when it comes to secondary data. It is a full-time job keeping up with the proliferation of sources of secondary data, and successful firms will hire librarians or outsource to consultants who can do this.

Provide Appropriate Consultation Services. Whether located in the market research area or the corporate library, one or more persons has to serve as a reference librarian: a person who can proactively help a manager find relevant resources rather than simply responding to queries. Inasmuch as most market research vendors award several hours of their analysts' time when reports are purchased, the reference librarian is also the logical choice to serve as gatekeeper to these analysts. Without a gatekeeper, the few hours of analyst time may be frittered away. Finally, whether in-house or outsourced, the library will want to make available a professional database searcher—someone who can execute effective search strategies of databases such as Dialog for minimum connect-time costs.

Bring the Library to the Desktop. Because more and more information is available in electronic form and because paper information is in any case a problem for multinational and decentralized firms, in the future most if not all of the corporate library will have to be made accessible from the desktop computer of the individual user. Major firms, such as Hewlett-Packard and Sun Microsystems, had already made substantial progress toward this goal by the end of 1994.

An important part of desktop access is proactive posting of information by the library to the individual user. Generally, a user will sign up for certain e-mail aliases (i.e., put him- or herself on the distribution list for certain kinds of e-mail), and the library will regularly pump out the appropriate information to the various aliases. This might include, for example, recent library acquisitions or types of bulletins now available.

Evaluate Sources of Information. Quality can vary dramatically across vendors and also within vendors depending on particular areas of expertise. It behooves any substantial purchaser of these reports to periodically evaluate the strengths and weaknesses of each research vendor based on past experience and to make these evaluations available for consultation by project, product, and program managers (Hewlett-Packard does this).

STEPS TO BE TAKEN FOR A
MARKET RESEARCH PROJECT

Identify Relevant Library Holdings. Early in the environment-scanning stage, you should budget some time for reading and browsing in the library. For example, you may try to construct graphs of trends in sales or market share by assembling a series of syndicated reports. For a second example, reading a set of reports interpreting industry events will help to constellate key issues in your mind.

Assemble Relevant Internal Secondary Data. Using data from within your firm, you may be able to produce illuminating breakdowns of where sales performance has been strong or weak, profiles of typical customer applications, segmentation analyses of your customer base, tabulations of reported problems and complaints, and so forth. If you can assemble past primary market research reports that address, however tangentially, your area of concern, then you may gain perspective beyond what you obtained from reading outside analysts' discussions.

Decide On a Search Strategy. If the scope of your project justifies it, you may want to mount a search of databases or sign up for a consultation with some market research analyst. You would go this route, for instance, if you were a product manager charged with preparing a backgrounder or white paper on whether the firm should expand into a particular market or pursue product development in a specific direction. In such instances, your responsibility is to pull together all the information available on this topic, and an effortful search strategy can be justified.

Decide Whether to Supplement the Available Secondary Data With Primary Market Research. Sometimes you will learn everything you need to know from secondary data, or more exactly, you will learn enough from secondary data that it would not be cost-effective to conduct additional primary market research. If you do decide to collect primary data, as you probably will in many cases, your definition of the problem and your research objectives will be much improved by your secondary research.

STEPS TO BE TAKEN FOR
ONGOING MARKET INTELLIGENCE

First, assume that you have a forward-looking corporate library as described earlier. The question becomes how to take best advantage of the ocean of available information that floods in on a weekly basis. You are not a librarian and neither are you an analyst who has the luxury of studying an industry or topic full-time. At most you can devote a few hours a week to library-based market intelligence gathering. That is really the first step: to commit a certain period of time—something you can reasonably hope to achieve in all but the hairiest week—to finding and reading materials that will add to your stock of marketing intelligence.

Second, sign up for the appropriate newsfeeds, bulletins, and e-mail aliases. Be familiar with the materials that can be sent to your desktop.

Flag articles that look interesting and read them. It helps a lot if there are certain times in your week when this kind of reading is easy rather than hard to do. Setting up good habits is half the battle.

Third, develop a personal clipping service or search profile. In a few years, this will be easy to do electronically; today, it remains an innovation and may or may not be possible at your firm. What you want is a set of key words or some more complicated search routine that can be run against a database on a periodic basis (once a month or once a quarter). The following are some examples that would be relevant for a typical product manager:

1. Mention of either of your two largest competitors or their important brands in any of several leading periodicals
2. Mention of the words *new* or *introduce* in conjunction with the name of your product category
3. Mention of any of the several major applications for your product (it will take practice to specify this search tightly enough)
4. Mention of the words *trend* with *market share, sales,* or *profit* in conjunction with your industry or product category

This kind of search will tend to yield articles that you really want to read, and receiving such highly relevant articles in turn reinforces the habit of making regular forays for market intelligence.

Fourth, build mental models of your markets. I would imagine that almost every product, project, and program manager already engages in a fair amount of reading. The point to remember is that you will read with greater understanding and enhanced recall if you *read actively*—meaning that you read with reference to mental models that you are trying to build, test, modify, or rebut. A manager once remarked to me that he thought the real shortcoming of American managers was that they did not put enough energy into constructing conceptual models of the driving forces and key factors within their industry. I have no way of proving or disproving this criticism. I do know that your reading will be more rewarding if it is done with reference to mental models you have built and modified over time.

In the market intelligence mode, it is best to keep these models simple and basic. I have in mind core statements that reflect what you think you know. The following are some examples in generic form:

1. Competitor X's biggest advantage is . . . Their biggest shortcoming is . . .
2. Customers of type Y place the greatest importance on . . .
3. There are Z major types of customers in this market. They are distinguished by . . .
4. Our major strengths in the marketplace are . . . Our significant weaknesses include . . .
5. Decision A was successful because . . . Decision B failed because . . .

Of course, the reality of professional life is that the activity of just reading is the kind of activity that inevitably drops toward the bottom of your "to do list." Searching for information that refines, deepens, or extends your model of "What's really going on" can be much more motivating.

Cost Factors

Subscriptions. Periodicals, digests, summaries, and the like will run from the low hundreds to the low thousands of dollars.

Syndicated reports. Depending on the size of the report and the difficulty of gathering the information therein, reports may cost anywhere from a few thousand to 10 or 20 thousand dollars.

Tracking studies. An investigation that is repeated periodically (an example would be store or warehouse audits conducted on a weekly or monthly basis) may cost many tens or hundreds of thousands per year.

Database search. Varies—typically there is a charge for connect time, if an on-line service is used, plus a charge for either the number of records searched or the number of hits from the search, plus printing charges.

Analyst time. Normal consulting rates are $75 to $200 per hour.

Examples

Because of the diversity of secondary research, some typical applications will be given in place of specific examples.

Sales and market share analysis. Analysts will compile data and do detective work to estimate market shares of key competitors, including breakdowns by application, by product subcategory, by region, by customer industry, and so forth. As part of this analysis, sales trends, including growth rates, will be discussed.

Trend analysis. Often the goal of a report is to go beyond collecting and reporting specific numbers to encompass interpretation and analysis of underlying dynamics, critical success factors, implications of recent events and decisions, and the like.

Customer segmentation. Reports may suggest a variety of schema for distinguishing and grouping various types of customers and discuss the particular needs and requirements of each segment.

Competitor analysis. Reports may dissect and critique business and marketing strategies of key competitors. Analyses will indicate strengths and weaknesses of products and describe markets in which each competitor enjoys advantages or suffers disadvantages.

Strengths and Weaknesses

An important strength of secondary research is that it is generally quickly available for a modest cost. This is no small advantage in many business situations. Moreover, as discussed earlier, it is difficult to do any kind of primary market research for less than $10,000. If a few days in the library can remove most of the key uncertainties about market facts, albeit without giving exact answers to all one's questions, this may save you tens of thousands of dollars. The key fact about secondary research, then, is that it already exists and is readily available. At a minimum, it can improve the focus of any primary research you do choose to conduct.

A particular advantage of *internal* secondary data is that it uses categories and breakdowns that reflect a corporation's preferred way of structuring the world. Outside analysts may use very different and not always comparable breakdowns. Internal databases will often contain very specific and detailed information and very fine-grained breakdowns. Finally, one can generally get a fairly good idea of the validity of the data because one can discuss how the data was gathered with the people responsible.

A particular strength of *external* secondary data is the objectivity of the outside perspective it provides. These reports are written by analysts with broad industry experience not beholden to any specific product vendor. Whereas a product manager has many responsibilities and may be new to the position, an analyst spends all of his or her time focusing on market trends or industry analysis.

A final advantage of specific instances of secondary data is that these may be the *only* available source of specific pieces of information. This is often true of government data, for instance. It would be impossible (and foolish) for any individual firm to attempt to match the efforts of the U.S. Bureau of the Census or Department of Commerce.

The most important weakness of secondary data is that they are gathered by other people for other purposes. Consequently, the data often do not quite exactly address your key question or concern. The answers, although not irrelevant, either lack specificity, use breakdowns that are not comparable to other data, or do not address key issues in enough depth or from the desired perspective. Sometimes this potential limitation is not a factor, as in cases in which the information you want is exactly the kind that secondary research is best suited to answer (e.g., aggregate market data). In other cases, particularly when customer requirements are a focal concern or when insight into the psychology and motivation of buying is crucial, secondary data may only scratch the surface.

Some external secondary data may be of suspect quality. One should never fall into the trap of assuming that a report, simply because it is well written and associated with a recognized consulting firm, offers some kind of window onto absolute truth. Quality varies—by analyst, by firm, by type of information, and by market category. Reports are prepared by people. These people may be very intelligent or less so, meticulous or sloppy, thorough or slapdash, well informed or full of unexamined assumptions. Most large buyers of secondary data develop a sense for which consulting firms are strong (or weak) in a particular area. This judgment may be explicit in documents prepared by corporate staff or implicit and locked in the heads of employees who work with these vendors on a regular basis. It behooves you to tap into this collective wisdom before spending large amounts of money or basing crucial decisions on a consulting firm's data. In general, when reviewing a report, you have to carefully examine its appendix describing the study methodology and come to your own judgment about study quality.

A weakness characteristic of internal secondary data, such as sales reports and customer databases, is that these describe only your *existing* customers. Do not assume that these data can be extrapolated to describe the market as a whole. Rather, there is every reason to believe that your customers do not exactly reproduce the characteristics of the total market.

Be careful of data that may be dated or too old. Technology markets often change rapidly. Finally, be aware that secondary data are less likely to exist outside the United States. Particularly in Asia and in developing countries, the secondary data that you would like to have and could reasonably expect to find in the United States simply may not exist.

Dos and Don'ts

Do ask your colleagues' opinions of specific vendors' performance.

Don't take numbers in syndicated reports at face value. Read the appendix and consider the methodology used. Pay particular attention to how samples were gathered and always maintain a healthy skepticism.

Do triangulate across vendors. Compare numbers gathered from different sources by different methods. Often the truth lies somewhere in between.

Don't try to absorb a mass of secondary data all at once. Develop habits of regular reading; keep a notebook devoted to insights, reminders, and mental notes about possible models.

Suggested Reading

American Marketing Association. (1994). *1994 Greenbook* (32nd ed.). New York: Author, New York Chapter, (212) 687-3280.

> This is the most comprehensive guide to market research suppliers and service providers, updated annually.

Herold, J. (1988). *Marketing and sales management: An information sourcebook.* Phoenix, AZ: Oryx.

> In addition to listing sources of market data, this source can serve as a supplement to Dickinson by providing leads to a broader literature, including topics such as advertising, personal selling, and sales promotion.

The life style market analyst 1995. (1995). Des Plaines, IL: SRDS.

Reddy, M. A., & Lazich, R. S. (1995). *World market share reporter.* New York: Gale Research.

> These are two examples of the wealth of published data available. Reddy and Lazich look at market shares for brands and products worldwide (a companion volume examines the United States), whereas the SRDS publication profiles each major city by the variety of lifestyle and demographic data.

Patzer, G. L. (1995). *Using secondary data in marketing research: United States and worldwide.* Wesport, CT: Quorum Books.

Stewart, D., & Kamins, M. (1992). *Secondary research: Information sources and methods* (2nd ed.). Newbury Park, CA: Sage.

> Both of these books provide a comprehensive guide to choosing and using secondary research. Stewart and Kamins have more extensive examples of the strategic use of this information, whereas Patzer adds an international focus.

Finally, all market research textbooks have a chapter on secondary research, and the most recent edition can be consulted for up-to-date lists of data sources. See, for example, pp. 318-335 of Churchill's text given in Chapter 2's Suggested Reading section.

4

Customer Visits

In a customer visit, one or more decision makers from a vendor directly interacts with one or more customers or potential customers of that vendor. Of course, salespeople and customer support personnel have such contacts daily with customers. For our purposes, however, a customer visit, considered as a kind of marketing intelligence or market research, specifically occurs when a decision maker from *outside* these areas interacts with customers. For example, research and development would not normally be considered a customer contact function. Consequently, when an engineer travels to a customer site, that is a customer visit. So also when a product marketer as opposed to a member of the field sales organization makes a presentation to customers or when a member of general management or someone in manufacturing or someone in quality travels to the customer site.

Note that the term *decision maker* is intended to be very general. It refers to anyone (not just upper management) who makes any kind of decision that affects customers. Thus, in new product development, design engineers are decision makers; in total quality efforts, manufacturing engineers and quality staff are decision makers; and in the design of marketing programs, marketing staff are decision makers. The term *customer* is intended to be similarly inclusive and encompasses present and potential customers, competitors' customers, internal-to-the-vendor customers, and key opinion leaders or influential personages who may shape customer buying decisions. Similarly, the individuals at customer firms who may participate in customer visits are not limited to purchasing agents, general management, or other traditional "vendor contact" positions but may include anyone who is involved in the consideration, buying, installation, maintenance, use, or disposal of the vendor's product.

Customer visits may be distinguished as *outbound*—where the vendor travels to the customer—or *inbound*—where the customer travels to the vendor site. Although we will focus on outbound visits that involve face-to-face contact, customer contacts via telephone or video conference also may be considered a kind of visit, as are face-to-face contacts that occur at neutral sites such as trade shows.

We can further distinguish *ad hoc* from *programmatic* customer visits. An ad hoc visit is any contact in which marketing research is *not* the primary agenda or driving force behind the visit but simply one of several motives. By contrast, a customer visit program consists of a series of visits that is conducted precisely to achieve some market research objective and in which market research is the primary and often the sole agenda. Recognize that ad hoc visits provide an important opportunity for marketing intelligence gathering, whereas programmatic visits can be considered as a market research technique just as focus groups, surveys, and experiments. Because the procedures are quite different in the two cases, ad hoc and programmatic visits will be discussed separately.

Ad Hoc Visits
for Marketing Intelligence

A truly astonishing number of ad hoc contacts with customers already occur. Engineers go on troubleshooting visits, product marketers give presentations explaining corporate strategy, managers make visits to support salespeople who are trying to close deals, customers come to the vendor for tours, and both parties meet at trade shows, for example. When I poll a group of a dozen managers on the number of such visits they and their direct reports will likely make next quarter, the number generally exceeds 100. What makes these visits "ad hoc" is that the primary agenda is to fix, to tell, or to sell, and not to learn. Moreover, at most firms today, these visits are planned and executed in isolation from one another. Each person conducts his or her own visits as the need arises, one by one, without coordination across individuals or over time.

Even more astonishing than the number and diversity of these ad hoc visits is that most firms do little to harvest marketing intelligence from them. For very little out-of-pocket cost, ad hoc visits could become a valuable source of insight into customer concerns, customer perspectives, and emerging market trends. Best of all, the effort to harness ad hoc visits would allow you to deliver customer and market information directly to a wide range of decision makers across functional areas in the organization. Five steps are required to achieve these benefits, as discussed in the following sections.

RESOLVE TO CHANGE

The present haphazard approach to nonprogrammatic visits evolved naturally over time in your organization. There is no reason to expect it to change overnight or without effort. For these visits to become an adjunct to marketing intelligence efforts, a manager or managers must commit to a change in habit, and this change in habit must be coordinated and sustained over time.

It is probably best to start small, at the business team or business unit level—or in some portion of a division. Call a meeting of the relevant players. Discuss the value of taking steps to move closer to customers. Finally—and it is this step that takes you beyond good intentions to an actionable plan—generate and agree on two to three perennial questions that everyone commits to asking during each ad hoc customer visit that occurs over the next quarter.

ARTICULATE PERENNIAL QUESTIONS

A perennial question is a general, discussion-starting query that can be asked of any customer with whom you happen to have 10 minutes. The following are some examples:

1. Why did you choose our product?
2. What is the worst difficulty you have in working with us?
3. What business problems are causing you to lose sleep?
4. How do you compare us with our competitors? What are our strengths and weaknesses?

Of course, you do not have to use any one of these examples. What you must do is come up with questions of this type that reflect your particular marketing intelligence needs of the moment. A good perennial question starts a discussion, opens avenues for exploration, and provides an opportunity to probe for details and clarification. A wide range of such questions may prove suitable from time to time. The important thing is that everyone commits to asking these questions at every opportunity.

LOG CUSTOMER PROFILES

If the articulation of perennial questions converts good intentions to action, it is the development of customer profiles that sustains that action. If you do not find some way to capture and record the results of asking perennial questions, then you have taken only a small step toward mastering the potential of ad hoc visits. With perennial questions alone, learning improves but retention may not, and sharing of learning is much less likely to occur.

The solution is to log the results of ad hoc visits in the form of a profile. This consists of a very brief document prepared immediately after the visit. (Brevity is important—multiplying onerous paperwork requirements is not the way to succeed in business in the 1990s.) The first part of the profile should be some kind of "header page" containing information of the sort normally maintained in customer databases: annual purchase volume, type of application, product configuration, and the like. The heart of the profile consists of the essence of the answers given by this customer to the perennial questions asked. Also important is the visitor's "takeaway"—any insights or impressions triggered by this visit. In sum, the profile documents the learning that occurred as a result of this visit.

REVIEW PROFILES

Thus far I have added coordination (perennial questions) and capture (profiles) to what had been thoroughly ad hoc visits. The next step is to promote sharing and discussion so that insights do not remain locked in the heads of individuals. A good way to do this is to call a meeting, after several months have elapsed, of all the people who committed to asking perennial questions. Prior to that meeting, make hard copies of all the profiles thus far accumulated and distribute them to all participants. Request that everyone read everyone else's profiles as preparation for the meeting. What happens now is that for the first time you see what other people have been hearing from customers. One customer answering one question constitutes a very weak data point; but now for the first time we have 30, 40, 60, or 80 customers, all of whom have been asked the same question. You may discover that an answer you received but thought was unusual or an exceptional case has in fact cropped up in several other profiles. Conclusion: Something is happening in the marketplace.

The purpose of this review meeting, then, is to compare notes; to reflect on patterns, trends, and puzzles; and in general, to answer the question, What are our customers trying to tell us? Out of the meeting will come understanding, a shared vision, and action plans. Not least, the meeting should consider whether the same or different perennial questions should be used going forward.

DATABASE VISITS AND PROFILES

The final step is to store a record of visits and profiles in some kind of database. Even a simple record of who visited whom and when would be invaluable in planning future ad hoc and programmatic visits. With such a record, anyone contemplating a customer visit easily could discover when this customer was last visited, who did the visit, and what issues emerged. Similarly, as more and more profiles accumulate, it becomes possible to do more interesting analyses of customer issues. Text retrieval software will allow a marketing strategist to search for any mention of competitor *X* or a design engineer to search for any mention of functionality *Y* or application *Z*. Moreover, managers planning programmatic customer visits can review profiles to determine likely candidates for inclusion.

SUMMARY

Better coordination of ongoing ad hoc customer visits costs very little money and promises a wealth of data on customer perceptions, feelings, and reactions. In contrast, most other forms of marketing intelligence emphasize more quantitative and factual kinds of data. There is also a secondary benefit of adding a learning objective to these visits. Customers are most accustomed to vendors whose primary mode of self-presentation is some version of, Can I sell you something today? You benefit from coming across also as a vendor who asks, Can I understand you a little better? Because long-term vendor-customer relationships are so crucial in many business-to-business and technology markets, this is no small benefit.

Programmatic Visits for Marketing Research

Some years ago, technology firms such as Hewlett-Packard began to experiment with a more systematic approach to customer visits in which 12, 20, or even 50 visits might be executed to address some topic of interest. The most common applications for such customer visit programs are new product development, new market development (i.e., selling an existing product line to a new type of customer or a new application), and customer satisfaction assessment. These programmatic visits are characterized by objectives set in advance, a carefully selected sample of customers, participation by cross-functional teams, a discussion guide used to direct the visit, an exploratory approach in asking questions, and a structured analysis and reporting process. What follows is an outline of the steps required to execute such a program.

SET OBJECTIVES

A program of visits tends to devolve into a series of ad hoc visits unless objectives are set in advance. Examples of feasible objectives would include the following:

Identify user needs.
Explore customer perceptions concerning market events or trends.
Generate ideas for product enhancement.
Describe how customers make their purchase decision.

These objectives should be hammered out in advance and regularly revisited. It is surprising how often the team of people who will participate in the visits does *not* initially agree on what the visits are supposed to accomplish. This occurs partly because customer visits are a highly flexible tool that can handle a wide variety of issues and partly because it is often the only marketing research technique over which participants have any direct control. Consequently, the visit program, unless checked, tends toward an "everything I wanted to know about customers but never had the chance to ask" orientation. For best results, remember that less is more: Fewer objectives, more thoroughly addressed, will generally be the best approach.

SELECT A SAMPLE

Sample selection is a make-or-break phase of program design. It does not matter how incisive your interviewing or insightful your analysis if you visit the wrong customers—people who do not deal with the issues that concern you or are not part of the market you are trying to address. Garbage in, garbage out is the rule.

Begin by reviewing any segmentation scheme used by your business. This review of segments is important because you probably want to visit multiple instances of each important or relevant type of customer *and* you want to avoid (for the visit program at hand) any kind of customer that is irrelevant to your objectives. For example, if your product is sold to four different industries, it may be important to visit customers from each; alternatively, if your product has a half dozen applications and the changes you are contemplating concern only three of these applications, then you may wish to include only customers with those applications in the sample. The end result of this first stage of sample selection is typically a list of 3 to 6 types of customers, yielding a tentative sample size of, in most cases, 12 to 36 visits (worldwide programs are generally somewhat larger, in the 30 to 60 range). In very concentrated markets, this list may name actual customer firms; in larger markets, it will be only a statement of types—that is, "national distributors with mainframe computers and a wide area network," "batch manufacturers with local area networks," and so forth.

The point of going through this exercise is to avoid first, the pitfalls of excluding customer types that are important to understand; second, wasting your time on customers who cannot really help you; and third (the most subtle trap), always returning to visit the same small group of comfortable, familiar customers. One firm that neglected this latter point watched their market share slowly shrink even as their customer satisfaction ratings continued to go up and up (because they were doing an ever-better job of satisfying an ever-smaller niche of the market). Often, the greatest discoveries and the most surprising insights will come from visits made to less familiar customers, such as competitors' customers, or to customers who spend a lot on this product category but not very much on your product offering (which implies that something about your product is lacking).

The second phase of sample selection is specifying which job roles at the customer firm you want to visit. Most business-to-business products are bought and used by means of a group decision-making process that involves multiple individuals. If you talk only to one role—or worse, to different roles at different customers, thus confounding interrole differences and interfirm differences—you risk coming to a partial and misleading perspective on your market. An important part of the recruiting process is qualifying the persons you will be interviewing at the customer site. It is extremely disappointing to fly at great time and expense to a customer site and realize, in the first 5 minutes, that you are speaking to someone who has no involvement with your issues. Because customer visits are one of the very few market research techniques that allow you to understand multiple decision makers at a customer site and because group decision making is so characteristic of business-to-business markets, most customer visits should include multiple job roles at each customer site. In many cases, this adds very little to the cost but substantially deepens the understanding gained. Recruiting itself can be handled by the program coordinator (common in concentrated markets with enduring vendor-customer relationships) or by an outside market research firm (common when customers are hard to find and also in close-to-mass-market situations with hundreds of thousands of buyers).

SELECT TEAMS

The best teams are cross-functional—one that includes someone from marketing plus someone from engineering (in the case of new product development) or someone from quality and someone from manufacturing engineering (in the case of customer satisfaction), for example. One reason for the superiority of teams is that a lot of work has to be done to make an interview effective and one person cannot do it all. A second reason is that cross-functional teams see with "stereo vision." Note that larger programs typically involve two or three teams to split up the workload so that no one team has to visit more than 6 to 10 customers.

DEVISE A DISCUSSION GUIDE

The guide is a two- to four-page document that functions as an agenda for the visit. In outline form, it lists the major topics to be covered and under each topic reminds you of key questions to be asked and issues to look out for. The topics are arranged in a sequence that will develop naturally and be comfortable for the customer. A discussion guide performs three valuable functions: It keeps you on track during each visit, it ensures consistency across visits, and it coordinates the efforts of multiple teams in large visits.

CONDUCT THE INTERVIEWS

You are *not* executing a survey in person; that is, you are not asking a fixed set of questions in a rigidly prescribed manner. Rather, you are engaged in a directed conversation with an expert informant—your customer. Exploration in depth is the focus. The two key skills to be mastered here are the creation of rapport and effective probing. You create rapport by demonstrating unconditional positive regard for the customer. Whether they deliver good news, bad news, or strange news, your attitude is constant: You are my customer, and it is important that I understand you. You do not need to "glad-hand" the customer, and you should not try to maintain a poker face. You need only come across as committed to listening and learning.

To probe means to ask follow-up questions to extend and clarify initial answers. In this connection, open-ended questions that do not prestructure answers should be emphasized in customer visits (i.e., "What are you looking for in your next printer?" as opposed to a closed-ended question such as, "Do you want two-sided printing in your next printer?"). Whenever you receive an answer to an open-ended question, your next question should almost invariably be some form of, "Anything else?" or "What else?" More generally, understand that customers, like other human beings, typically give vague, nonspecific, rambling, semicoherent answers to questions. To fully grasp the meaning of these answers requires effective probing.

DEBRIEF THE TEAMS

Immediately after concluding the visit, it is important that the team debriefs. In the beginning of the visit program, debriefing provides an opportunity to discuss changes to the discussion guide and interview procedure. Toward the conclusion, debriefing gives you a head start on the analysis, as you ask how today's visit compares and contrasts with previous visits. Throughout, debriefing provides a cross-check on each team member's perceptions of what customers are saying.

ANALYZE AND REPORT RESULTS

Analysis can be free-form or structured. In free-form analysis, a review of visit notes uncovers themes, contrasts, discoveries, and enumerations (i.e., customer needs or requirements identified through the visits). An example of a structured approach would be *quality function deployment* (QFD). Here matrices are generated to map customer requirements onto product features and engineering criteria.

It is fair to say that the quality of analysis of customer visit data depends heavily on the insight and industry experience of the person(s) analyzing the visit. Although no kind of market research ever eliminates the need for judgment and perspective, this need is particularly great in the case of customer visits.

Examples

The following are two examples of visit programs—one conducted by Sun Microsystems to better understand sources of customer satisfaction and dissatisfaction and the other conducted by Apple Computer to explore the potential for a new product.

Sun Microsystems wanted to understand problems associated with a customer's "first encounter" with the company, specifically, from the point where the shipment of computers first arrived until the system was up and running. This effort was spearheaded by members of the company's quality function who perceived that the first encounter was sometimes more problematic than it had to be. Cross-functional teams conducted more than 50 visits worldwide, yielding a variety of insights that would have been difficult or impossible to obtain in any other way. These ranged from the impact of the packaging used, to international differences in desk layout and office configuration, to subtle problems with the usability and installation of various pieces of equipment. Because solutions to many of these problems cut across departments and functions, the cross-functional makeup of the visit teams proved crucial in addressing identified problems.

The Display Products Division of Apple Computer wanted to explore the potential for an entirely new product category that would expand the division's offerings. The goal of the visit program was to discover unmet needs that present products did not satisfy, to describe customer requirements that the new product would have to meet, and to explore the fit between Apple's core competency and these requirements.

The division conducted more than 30 visits in the United States and Europe. A product manager from the marketing function coordinated the visits, and a wide range of scientists and engineers participated (the new product solution was much more than an incremental change or twist on an existing offering). Marketing managers combined information gained from these visits with secondary and other market research to help division management understand the issues surrounding the decision whether to invest in the new solution.

The visits yielded a wealth of data, summarized in profiles, about applications for the new product, problems with existing solutions, and perceptions of Apple's ability to deliver a successful solution. Design engineers came away from the visits with a clear vision of what the product had to do to succeed.

Cost

A good estimating procedure is to multiply the number of visits contemplated by $1,000 to account for direct travel costs incurred by a two-person team (airfare, hotel, car rental, and meals). Programs with a substantial international component will cost more; on the other hand, programs in which all the visits are conducted locally by car will have negligible out-of-pocket costs. Purely local programs generally are not a good idea, however, because your mental models probably are already overly shaped by local customers and because there is often considerable geographical diversity in customer viewpoints, inasmuch as different industries are concentrated in different locales. One approach to controlling costs for out-of-town visits is to bunch several visits onto a single airfare, inasmuch as airfare is often the largest component of travel expense. Another is to piggyback research visits onto existing trips: If you are already scheduled to go to Atlanta for a conference, why not stay an extra day or two and conduct several visits as part of a program that will span a month or two?

Strengths and Weaknesses

The customer visit technique has several key strengths that combine to position visits just behind secondary research as a general all-purpose market research tool. First, visits are field research—they take you out of your world and put you into the customer's world. Second, visits take the form of face-to-face interaction. Research has shown that face-to-face is the richest of all communication modes, in the sense of being best able to handle complex, ambiguous, and novel information. Third, the combination of field study and face-to-face communication is ideal for entering into the customer's thought world—the customer's perspective and priorities. Being able to think like a customer is perhaps the core marketing competency, and customer visits provide one of the best means of helping nonmarketing functions such as engineering to envision their customers. Fourth, customer visits provide information that is gained firsthand, directly. As someone remarked to me, "Everyone believes his or her own eyes and ears over others." Customer visits can sometimes be helpful in changing hearts and minds because the evidence of an unsatisfied need is so much more vivid and compelling when gathered this way. Overall, the distinctive strength of customer visits is depth of understanding. For instance, you can spend a whole hour nailing down exactly what goes on in a particular application or process. Sustained dialogue gives you the picture seen from multiple reinforcing angles, in a way that a table of cross-tabulated survey responses never will.

The great weakness of customer visits is the potential for interviewer bias. If you have spent 6 months slaving over a design concept, will you really be able to listen to and explore the response of that customer whose initial reaction is something along the lines of "What a silly idea"? Historically, the consensus of academic opinion was that managers could not be trusted to conduct their own market research; rather, the combination of greater objectivity and expertise made outside professionals the superior choice. Perhaps a more balanced perspective would be that although bias is a constant danger, nonetheless, the potential advantages compel the involvement of managers and other decision makers in customer visits. Given this realization, one can act to control bias in two ways: first by the use of teams (although my bias is invisible to me, it will be painfully apparent to you!) and second by following up customer visits with other more controlled procedures, such as survey research, choice modeling, and experimentation.

The second abiding weakness of customer visits is the instability and imprecision consequent to small sample sizes. Often there is a great temptation to treat a customer visit program as a kind of survey and to report findings such as, "75% of our customers had a positive reaction to adding this piece of functionality" or "Only 1 customer in 8 reported having problems with X." Just a little statistical reflection will reveal that in a random sample of 16 customers, the 95% confidence interval around an estimate of "75% agreement" extends from 53% to 97%; in the nonrandom samples typically used for customer visits, this confidence interval must be wider still. If you want the kind of precision that percentages imply, you need a large sample survey. Where customer visits excel is in explaining *why* some customers had a favorable reaction to a piece of functionality, not in estimating the proportion of customers who have that reaction.

Dos and Don'ts

Do get engineers and other nonmarketers involved in customer visits.

Don't confine yourself to a conference room. Walk around and observe. Soak up the total picture of this customer's operation.

Do enlist the support and cooperation of the local field sales organization. They can do so much to frustrate or assist your purpose. They know these customers well and can add perspective to what you hear.

Don't ask customers for solutions—ask them to identify problems that need solving. The customer is the authority on what the real problems are, but the vendor is the authority on what a profitable solution to those problems might be.

Don't talk too much. You are there to listen. The more you talk, the more you shape customer responses and the less your chances of making a discovery or being surprised.

Do use visual aids. Diagrams, short lists, and the like help the customer to focus on the total idea to which you want reactions.

Do use verbatim quotes from customers in reports. Customers often express themselves more vividly and with less inhibition than you would allow yourself.

Suggested Reading

Bailetti, A. J., & Guild, P. D. (1991). Designer's impressions of direct contact between product designers and champions of innovation. *Journal of Product Innovation Management, 8,* 91-103.

> This academic study describes the impact of participation in a customer visit program for design engineers for a telecommunications project.

Griffin, A., & Hauser, J. R. (1992). *The voice of the customer* (Report No. 92-106). Cambridge, MA: Marketing Science Institute.

> This report addresses a number of issues associated with conducting customer visits, in particular, the necessary sample size.

Guillart, F. J., & Sturdivant, F. D. (1994). Spend a day in the life of your customer. *Harvard Business Review, 72,* 116-125.

> These authors describe some uses of inbound customer visits and clarify the kind of perspective customers are uniquely qualified to give.

McQuarrie, E. F. (1993). *Customer visits: Building a better market focus.* Newbury Park, CA: Sage.

> I provide a complete step-by-step guide to designing, conducting, and analyzing a program of visits.

McQuarrie, E. F. (1995). Taking a road trip: Customer visits help companies recharge relationships and pass competitors. *Marketing Management, 3,* 8-21.

> Where my book concentrates on programmatic customer visits, this article expands on applications of customer visits to marketing intelligence.

Miles, M. B., & Huberman, A. M. (1994). *Qualitative data analysis: An expanded sourcebook.* Thousand Oaks, CA: Sage.

Weitzman, E. A., & Miles, M. B. (1995). *Computer programs for qualitative data analysis: A software sourcebook.* Thousand Oaks, CA: Sage.

> These two books address the issue of what to do with customer visit data once you obtain it. Miles and Huberman provide an authoritative account of analysis approaches, whereas Weitzman and Miles explain how computers can assist in such analysis.

Shapiro, B. (1988). What the hell is "market-oriented"? *Harvard Business Review, 66,* 119-125.

> Shapiro shows how customer visits can be used to turn around a stagnant organization and make it more market focused.

von Hippel, E. (1990). *The sources of innovation.* New York: Oxford University Press.

> Von Hippel describes what can be learned from visits to lead users—creative, knowledgeable customers who are adapting existing products to novel uses.

5

The Focus Group

The term *focus group* often is used loosely to cover any group interview. Strictly speaking, however, in the world of market research, a focus group is a particular kind of group interview supported by a specialized infrastructure. This infrastructure includes (a) the facility, (b) the market research vendor, and (c) the moderator.

The facility is an independent small business that has at least one specialized meeting room. This room will have a table capable of seating a dozen consumers, a one-way mirror from behind which observers can view the proceedings, and the capacity to audio- and videotape the group. The facility typically will be located in a shopping mall or office building.

The market research vendor is generally a separate business entity responsible for coordinating the entire focus group research project. The three specific responsibilities of the vendor are to find a facility, supply a moderator who will lead the groups, and arrange for consumers to be recruited to attend (both the moderator and the recruiter may themselves be separate business entities and often the facility will handle recruiting in addition to hosting the group). The value added by the vendor is fundamentally that provided by any middleman or broker: The vendor consults with you to design an appropriate research strategy, brings together all the resources required to implement the study, and then drives the process to its conclusion.

The moderator is an individual with general skills in conducting an interview and specific skills in managing group interaction. Virtually all focus group moderators also conduct one-on-one interviews, but not all people who conduct one-on-one interviews are capable of running a focus group. Interviewing a group is more demanding. In addition to leading the group, the moderator will work with the client before the group to refine the objectives for the discussion and will typically but not always be the analyst who writes the report on the groups (some vendors separate the moderating and analysis tasks).

If this infrastructure is not present, it is probably best to refer to your research study as simply a group interview to avoid confusion.

Procedure

1. You send out a request for proposals (RFP) to several market research vendors outlining the kind of customers you want recruited, the number of groups to be held (three or four is typical), and the issues and topics to be explored in the group.

2. The selected vendor recommends a facility (often, groups will be held in two or more cities to encompass regional differences in consumer response), puts you in touch with a moderator, and prepares for your review the screener that will be used by phone recruiters.

3. You edit the screener, which consists of four to five questions designed to make sure that the consumers who are recruited are in fact the right kind of people for your purposes. For example, if you are a computer manufacturer exploring the needs of computer users who work at home, the screener will be designed to ensure that each participant (a) does work at home for some minimum number of hours, (b) does have a computer, and (c) does use that computer as part of working at home. The screener

might also ensure that one or more applications is present—that is, that a spreadsheet is used. Finally, the screener might be used to build a mix into the group: to recruit 3 to 4 users of DOS, 3 to 4 users of Windows, and 2 to 3 Apple Macintosh users as part of an 8- to 10-person focus group.

4. Phone recruiting commences. Many calls have to be made to get a person on the line; some of these people prove to be ineligible, and some of the remaining are not interested. As recruiting proceeds, you review the completed screeners to make sure the right kinds of people are being recruited.

5. Meanwhile, you meet with the moderator to develop the discussion guide. Typically, you have written a memo describing the topics and issues to be raised in the group discussion and some specific questions to be asked. The moderator transforms this into a discussion guide that functions as an agenda for the group. Specifically, the discussion guide indicates how topics will be sequenced and how questions will be worded.

6. You and any of your colleagues who will be attending the focus group meet with the moderator at the facility 1 hour before the group is scheduled to begin. As consumers arrive, you stay in touch with the facility host or hostess to double check eligibility and to make snap decisions about who to include if a surplus of people actually shows. Consumers are generally served food while they wait.

7. The group itself will last 1.5 to 2 hours. You have the opportunity to send in one or two notes and to huddle briefly with the moderator before the wrap up. After each group (two will generally be held in an evening), alterations can be made to the discussion guide.

8. After the last group, the moderator or analyst spends 1 to 3 weeks preparing a report. These vary in length according to what you are willing to pay. Longer reports will contain verbatim quotes drawn from the tapes. You also may choose to have a summary videotape made that contains 10 to 15 minutes of particularly insightful discussion.

Cost Factors

For business-to-business groups, budget for $4,000 to $9,000 per group and a three-group minimum. It is a rare project that includes more than six groups, so you can assume that most focus group projects will cost between $15,000 and $50,000. The breakdown of costs is roughly as follows:

Facility: $300 to $500 per group

Recruitment: Depends on difficulty of finding people—generally the single biggest cost factor

Moderator: $1,000 per group and up, depending on type of report

Participant fees: About $50 per participant for an ordinary professional (e.g., engineer), $100 for managers and people in high demand (e.g., MIS directors), greater than $100 for executives, doctors, and the like

Videotaping: $500 per group

Food: $5 to $15 per participant

Vendor overhead: Varies

Examples

The first example is a business that made small hand-held testing equipment used by customers whose factories manufactured a variety of electrical systems. The product in question was one among many made by the business, and this business unit in turn was part of a large, well-known, multinational firm. Although the product had been offered for decades in one form or another, it had never been the leading brand in its market.

A strategic review indicated it was time to develop a new generation of the product to reflect advances in technology. Product marketing staff argued for focus groups as an initial stage of market research. The staff pointed out that objective measures of product performance and business strength did not square with the product's weak market position. Something else had to be going on, and if the next generation of the product was to succeed, this "something else" had to be understood.

Four focus groups were conducted with technicians and engineers who used this product in the course of their work. The screeners used in recruitment ensured that users of several brands, including the company's own, were present. Given the firm's weak position in the market, however, a majority of those who attended were users of other brands. The use of an outside research vendor ensured that the sponsoring firm remained anonymous. This contributed to a frank and candid atmosphere in the groups.

The group discussions, which were viewed by marketing staff and engineering management, had the effect of a bucket of cold water. Some quite harsh and belittling comments were made about the sponsor and its product. Comments such as "Overengineered and overpriced" and "Way too delicate for use on the factory floor" give some indication of the tone. Intriguingly, the charge of fragility had no basis in objective fact. Engineering analyses had shown the product to be no less sturdy or durable than its competitors. Rather, fragility was an inference made by potential customers based on how the product's casing looked and felt.

The focus groups had a salutary effect on management—a "wake-up call" as one marketer put it. A 15-minute video containing highlights was widely shown and had a galvanizing effect. Both customer visits and a descriptive survey were subsequently undertaken to extend and confirm the results of the focus group. The new product designed in light of this research was extremely successful in the marketplace, with the result that the leading brand lost a substantial chunk of its market share—so much so that the competitor fired the manager of its product line on the theory that only managerial incompetence could explain such a drastic loss of share!

The company providing the second example is a large computer manufacturer that undertook research in the late 1980s to better understand the issue of software quality. Although the firm had always had a commitment to making high-quality products, the growing importance of software to its revenue stream, in combination with the emerging emphasis on *total quality*, suggested a need for exploratory market research. In particular, corporate quality staff had the uneasy sense that quality had come to be too narrowly defined as errors per line of code and was seeking to understand the customer's perspective on the meaning of quality.

Eight focus groups were conducted as part of what was intended to be a two-stage research project, in which the second stage would be a large-scale choice modeling study designed to identify the importance of each of the quality attributes identified in the focus groups. Although some members of the corporate market research staff had wanted to move immediately to the choice modeling study, quality staff insisted on doing focus groups first, out of a sense that too many issues remained undefined.

Two groups each were conducted in Boston, New York, Atlanta, and San Francisco. Four groups concerned engineering or technical software applications (e.g., computer-aided design), and four groups concerned general commercial applications (e.g., word processing, accounting). For both the commercial and engineering software sets, two groups consisted of ordinary software users, one group consisted of MIS directors responsible for supporting such users, and one group consisted of independent software consultants and software suppliers. Screening during recruitment ensured that users of large and small computers, users of the firm's own software and other brands, and employees of large and small businesses would be included.

The groups proved valuable in several respects. First, the customer perspective on quality became much more richly articulated. Diverse attributes of quality, such as "robust" and "intuitive," which had been little more than catch phrases before, were elaborated with examples, clarifications, and contrasts. Second, the term *software quality* proved to hold virtually no meaning for the typical user. Blank stares were a typical reaction when the moderator introduced this term in the early groups. Components of the software product, such as manuals or help screens, sometimes elicited energetic discussion of good or bad, but software quality per se was not a concept that users could define easily. Third, likes and dislikes proved very heterogeneous across users—whatever software quality was, it was not one unvarying thing. Fourth, and most important, most users were familiar with only one brand of software—the one they used. Competitive products had essentially no visibility in most cases.

As a result of the groups, the choice modeling study was canceled. The particular choice modeling technique under consideration required ratings of competitor products—a task that would clearly be impossible for users in light of the focus group discussions. Consequently, the focus group project yielded two benefits. The corporate quality staff's understanding of software quality from the customer's perspective was greatly enriched and an expensive and ill-advised quantitative market research study, costing upward of $80,000, was avoided.

Strengths and Weaknesses

The great strength of the focus group technique is its capacity to produce surprise and a fresh perspective. Because the interview is minimally structured, because participants react to and provoke one another, and because the moderator drives the group to reflect and explore, there is a high probability that management will hear something new and unexpected. Hence, focus groups make a great deal of sense *early* in a market research project.

The unique strength of the focus group is that it brings multiple customers into direct interaction with one another. It is customary to extol the "synergy" that results. This rather vague term, however, can be given a much more precise definition drawing on theories from social psychology. Two fundamental processes occur in discussion groups composed of strangers: Groups *unify* and groups *polarize.* Initially, strangers seek common ground; subsequently, they polarize into factions.

This twin dynamic has powerful implications for market research using focus groups. Because of the unification dynamic, focus groups are very useful when exploring a new market or getting back in touch with an old market. Thus, if you are a computer company that is expanding into a hospital market and you convene a focus group of 10 nurses, these nurses will re-create "nurse world" within the group. The unification dynamic makes the *common denominator* visible. Because of the polarization dynamic, focus groups also are useful in identifying possible segment boundaries. In the process of dividing into factions, customers in the group will reveal what makes them *different* from one another. This is helpful because it prevents premature closure—you discover that one size will not fit all. Focus groups may be the only market research technique in which customers challenge one another, argue, and dissent in ways that an interviewer would never dare. This can reveal the extent to which people are committed to diverse views.

Finally, focus groups have a number of minor advantages that can be useful in certain circumstances. In the United States at least, the identity of the sponsor need not be revealed to participants (this is not always the case overseas). This can be most useful when you want to hear frank and candid assessments of your brand as compared to others. Customer visits—the major alternative to focus groups when exploratory research is desired—do not enjoy this advantage. Another useful feature is that focus groups occur in a concentrated time interval. A busy high-level manager is much more likely to show up for two evenings and thus view four focus groups than she or he is to accompany you on the week of travel required to make six customer visits. Because the focus group can be unobtrusively videotaped, you can, by creating and circulating an edited "highlights" tape, expose a large number of employees to almost direct customer input.

The most important weakness of the focus group technique is one that it shares with customer visits and other exploratory tools—the reliance on small, nonrandom samples. Because the sample is small and may or may not reflect the larger population of consumers in the market, the kinds of conclusions you can draw from focus group research are limited. You can *never* confidently extrapolate a percentage or frequency from a group. Thus, it is never appropriate to conclude from groups that "consumers preferred Concept A to Concept B by a 2-to-1 margin." Note that this difficulty does not in any way diminish if one adopts a loose and imprecise manner of speaking. "Only a few consumers see problems with . . ." is just as illegitimate an extrapolation as "Only 12% of consumers see problems with . . ." The judgment "only a few" draws exactly the same quantitative inference from the focus group sample as "only 12%." Neither is justified when the representativeness of the sample is unknown.

It might be objected, "Well, what good are focus groups, then?" Although focus groups can never estimate the *frequency* of some consumer judgment, preference, or response, they can reveal the fact of its existence and illuminate its nature. To refer back to the first example application given earlier, the focus group revealed that one or more real customers believed that the product was overengineered and overpriced and that some viewed it to be fragile. Ensuing discussion also revealed possible sources for such beliefs and their position within the network of other beliefs. However, were these beliefs held by a *few* idiosyncratic customers, by *some group* of customers, or by *many* customers? There was no way to know until follow-up research was conducted. All management could know based on groups alone was the nature and character of those beliefs, together with the knowledge that at least *some* customers held them. If those beliefs and their exact nature came as a surprise, then the groups paid for themselves. If managers had already known (and taken seriously) all these things, then the groups would have proved a waste of time.

Focus groups suffer from a number of other weaknesses that are distinctive and not shared with other kinds of exploratory research. Most of these stem from the very fact that a group is involved. Specifically, focus groups are quite vulnerable to logistical foul-ups. Traffic jams, random events, customers' busy schedules, and so forth may produce a higher-than-expected number of no-shows. It is hard to do a focus group when only three people actually show. Worse—most of the money spent is irretrievably lost.

More generally, focus groups are vulnerable to dominant individuals who monopolize the conversation, to shy individuals who withdraw, and to bandwagon effects in which group members simply acquiesce with an initial vehemently stated position. A good moderator can control many of these effects, but they remain liabilities.

The group synergy characteristic of focus groups also has a downside: limits on airtime. In a 2-hour group with eight people, an average of 15 minutes of airtime is available to each person. Can you learn everything you need to know from an individual customer in 15 minutes? For many relatively simple consumer products, the answer may well be yes; for business-to-business and technology products, the answer may be no, in which case, customer visits should be examined as an alternative. Also because of airtime restrictions, focus groups are an inferior idea-generation technique. Research has shown that interviews with 32 individuals will yield more and better ideas than 4 focus groups with 8 people each. Of course, focus groups may be a *satisfactory* idea-generation technique, even though not a superior one (especially given the time savings associated with conducting 4 groups versus 32 individual interviews). But focus groups are probably better suited to examining a few key topics in depth rather than generating a wide variety of ideas.

Finally, the use of a professional moderator is both a strength and a weakness. The moderator contributes interviewing skills plus detachment and objectivity. The downside, for many technology and business-to-business marketers, concerns the moderator's ability to quickly assimilate the essentials of your business situation and the technical specifics of your product. Absent that understanding, the moderator is not going to be able to effectively probe topics raised in the groups. In the fact that the profession of moderator continues to exist suggests that individuals who take this career path tend to be quick studies who can assimilate the necessary knowledge, client after client. On the other hand, the complexity of some technology products is such that I have encountered businesses that have soured on focus groups precisely because of their experiences with moderators who could not effectively probe key issues. If your product fits this profile, it is crucial that you feel comfortable that the moderator you intend to use has the requisite understanding. Customer visits are a fallback technique if you lack that confidence.

Dos and Don'ts

Do invite key players in different functional areas to view the groups. Much important thinking and discussion occurs behind the one-way mirror.

Do monitor the telephone screening of potential participants. Look at the completed screeners and ask yourself if this is in fact the kind of person you are hoping will attend.

Do evaluate the moderator—so much depends on this person's skill.

Don't count responses. Do not take votes seriously. (Votes are okay as a springboard for further discussion. It is when you draw inferences based on the vote that the trouble begins.)

Don't distribute and analyze questionnaires. It is okay to get additional background information to help interpret the responses of participants, but it is not okay to treat the people who happen to attend the groups as grist for an almost free survey.

Don't stop with one group or two. If focus groups are worth doing at all, you should do three or more.

Don't make the recruiting parameters too ambitious. This drives up the cost and may cause recruiting to fail altogether. It also suggests that you are seeking a precision that focus groups cannot give.

Suggested Reading

Goldman, A. E., & McDonald, S. S. (1987). *The group depth interview: Principles and practice.* New York: Prentice Hall.

> Goldman and McDonald provide an excellent resource for moderators who want to improve their skills. If you are a person who will have occasion to conduct group interviews from time to time, you also will find useful advice. They are particularly strong on the psychological aspects of group interviews.

Greenbaum, T. (1993). *The handbook for focus group research* (rev. and expanded ed.). Lexington, MA: Lexington Books.

> This is probably the best book for the businessperson who will use focus groups for purposes of making a business decision. Greenbaum covers the whole phenomenon and has some particularly interesting chapters on future trends and careers as a focus group moderator.

Krueger, R. A. (1994). *Focus groups: A practical guide for applied research* (2nd ed.). Thousand Oaks, CA: Sage.

> Krueger addresses the special case of service providers and nonprofit organizations that may choose to conduct focus groups.

Morgan, D. L. (1988). *Focus groups as qualitative research.* Newbury Park, CA: Sage.

> Morgan, a sociologist, addresses a different audience from that of the other books named: scholars who will use focus groups as part of their scholarship. This is useful as an assignment to students who will conduct focus groups as part of a research project. Because Morgan disdains the need for the infrastructure described at the beginning of the chapter, the book is also useful to those who, for cost or other reasons, will not have access to that infrastructure.

Stewart, D. W., & Shamdasani, P. N. (1990). *Focus groups: Theory and practice.* Newbury
   Park, CA: Sage.

   This is a good choice for a supplemental reading in a seminar on market
   research methods. Stewart and Shamdasani integrate focus group practice
   with the extensive social psychological literature on small-group behavior.

6

Survey Research

The broad term *survey* can be applied to any procedure in which a fixed set of questions is asked of a sample of respondents. In the case of most surveys, both the list of questions to be asked and the answer categories to be used with each question will be specified in advance. Moreover, the sample of respondents generally will be large and intended to represent a population with specific characteristics—for example, individuals who use a computer at home, software engineers who use the C+ programming language, or MIS directors who primarily use IBM equipment. "Large" means that sample sizes are rarely less than 100 and often exceed 1,000.

Surveys can be administered in person (somewhat rare), by telephone (the most common method in contemporary market research), by mail (not uncommon but not preferred), and by e-mail or other electronic means (growing in popularity). For purposes of this chapter, *survey* will more particularly mean a descriptive survey: a set of questions designed to describe a state of affairs in which the typical result takes the form of either a percentage figure (e.g., "35% of home computer users have enrolled in one or more on-line services"), a frequency count (e.g., "On average, C+ programmers make one call per month to software vendors' technical support lines"), or a cross-tabulation or group comparison (e.g., "28% of MIS directors with exclusively IBM mainframes reacted favorably to this proposal, as compared to 47% of MIS directors having both IBM and non-IBM mainframes in their shop"). Note that some implementations of some other kinds of market research procedures (notably choice modeling and controlled experiments) also may use questionnaires and large samples, but their purpose is very different—that is, to model a choice process or determine a causal sequence. Consequently, it is best to keep these procedures mentally separate from the kinds of procedures described in this chapter in which the focus is on *descriptive* surveys. For convenience, I will concentrate on telephone and mail surveys in that these means of administration continue to make up the bulk of market research applications.

The survey is the most familiar of all market research methodologies. Virtually every adult reading this book will have been on the receiving end of some kind of survey: a phone call at home, a letter in the mail, or a person with a clipboard in a mall. Moreover, it is a rare business student today who completes an undergraduate or graduate degree in business without having occasion to design, conduct, and analyze at least one survey. This familiarity, combined with the incredible ease with which a bad survey can be initiated and completed and in conjunction with the comfort that comes from obtaining seemingly precise numerical data, creates a problem: There are almost certainly too many surveys being done in market research today. By this I mean that some portion of the effort put into surveys would be more productive if invested instead in either choice modeling and controlled experiments on the one hand, or customer visits and focus groups on the other. In fact, for the managerial reader of this chapter, I would be quite happy if it served as a bucket of cold water. Surveys can be enormously expensive, and if this chapter causes you to question whether your current level of expenditure on surveys is ill-considered, then it has partly served its purpose. The number of cases in business in which it is worthwhile to spend a substantial amount of money to estimate precisely some percentage or frequency, and only that, is limited. If such descriptive precision is really your goal, then, of course, the survey is the tool of choice; when it is not, then the survey may be a poor use of resources indeed.

Procedure

It is quite possible (although not always advisable) to conduct a survey yourself; alternatively, you can hire a vendor to do it for you. Survey research is a mainstay of many market research firms, and there is no shortage of assistance available. Whereas focus groups are somewhat of a specialty item, and choice modeling even more so, virtually every market research vendor, large or small, conducts surveys. In what follows, the procedure for conducting a survey with a vendor's help is described. Issues involved in conducting your own survey are summarized later in this section.

STEP 1

You prepare a request for proposals (RFP) that outlines the characteristics of the population you want to survey (e.g., female heads of household who own cellular phones), the kinds of information you want to obtain, and the purpose of gathering this information (e.g., to describe current patterns of usage of cellular phones so as to prepare for the design of new calling plans targeted at this population). In the RFP, you also will want to give some indication of the desired sample size and the source of the sample (e.g., a list provided by you, a list bought by the vendor, or a random calling procedure), as these are important cost factors. Alternatively, as part of their proposal, vendors may propose solutions to these issues based on their expertise.

You also will have to indicate in the RFP how the survey is to be administered. The default choice is the telephone: It is quicker, it is cost-effective, and it has a much higher response rate than mail administration. There are some situations, however, that may require a mail questionnaire, as when questions are lengthy, complex, or numerous or when they require visual stimuli. People can process much greater amounts of information and more complex information by reading as opposed to listening, and if your survey has that kind of complexity, then mail administration may be a superior means of administration. Do ask your vendor for advice on this point.

STEP 2

The selected vendor will work with you to hammer out the text of the questions and the answer categories to be used in the survey. You can expect the vendor to have expertise in the area of question phrasing, knowledge concerning effective types of questions, and ideas about how best to sequence questions. Specifically, the vendor will advise you on how to phrase questions to obtain the highest quality information and which sequences are least likely to alienate the respondent or lead to premature termination. These are specialized technical skills and part of the vendor's stock-in-trade. Your task as the client is to be very clear about what kind of information you need. This in turn is a function of carefully considering your research objectives as discussed in previous chapters. In addition, the more preparatory research you have done the more guidance you will be able to give the vendor about the language that customers in this market actually use, the issues that really concern them, and the range of possible answers. Most surveys contain only a small number of nondirective, exploratory, open-ended questions. Instead, most of the questions will be very specific (e.g., "Which of the following parties do you call more often than once a month from your car?"), as will the answer categories (e.g., spouse, child, other relative, physician, neighbor, school, employer, employee). If you have not done the preparatory work to get the lay of the land via secondary research, focus groups, customer visits, and the like, then you probably are not ready to do a survey. Of course, something can always be cobbled together—you are knowledgeable about your industry, plus the vendor has plenty of canned examples—but will that survey be any good?

You can expect the construction of the survey questions to be an iterative process with many faxes sent back and forth. More minds are definitely better here, and you should get teammates, influential decision makers, and anyone else whose opinion you respect to read and comment on early drafts. It is amazing how often a question that seemed entirely unproblematic to you while sitting in your office will prove to contain an ambiguity, an unfortunate connotation, or a significant risk of miscomprehension. In addition, circulating the questionnaire and allowing people to influence its content build buy-in across the organization, which in turn enhances the likelihood that the results will be heeded in subsequent decision making.

STEP 3

You and the vendor decide on the size and the source of the sample. The size of the sample is dictated by the precision of the answers you require. If you want to know, to within ± 3 percentage points, the percentage of software engineers who have encountered a particular bug, then you will need a fairly large sample; if you would be satisfied with an estimate to within ± 8 percentage points, then a smaller sample will be adequate. There is no mystery to setting sample size—well-accepted statistical formulas exist. These formulas work best, however, when you can provide some prior information to the vendor, such as whether this bug is believed to be fairly rare or fairly common. Your vendor will also probably have rules of thumb about sample size based on past experience with surveys of this type. Remember that it is your prerogative as the paying customer to ask for an explanation of how sample size was determined. If you get an evasive answer or you cannot understand the answer, that is a bad sign. The mathematics of sample size selection is straightforward and should be well within your vendor's competence.

The source of the sample generally will be either a list that you provide, a list that the vendor buys, or some kind of random sampling process, such as random digit dialing. In random digit dialing, phone numbers to be called are generated by a computer. The process of number generation anticipates and allows for a fair number of dud calls (e.g., businesses, numbers not in service). The rationale for random digit dialing is that many people have unlisted phone numbers and people with unlisted numbers may differ in significant ways from those with listed numbers. Plus, a preexisting list cannot always be found.

The audience for this book—business-to-business and technology firms—is less likely to use random digit dialing, which is primarily important in mass consumer markets. Instead, you will almost always be working from some kind of list. If you can supply the list and if it is a good list in the sense of having few duds (e.g., names of people who have moved, changed jobs, or do not fit the population), then the cost of your survey research will be substantially less. If the vendor has to buy multiple lists or if there are no good lists available, then the cost goes up accordingly. The list industry is huge and growing, and some kind of list generally can be obtained, but cost goes up with the rarity and inaccessibility of the sample sought.

The most important thing to remember is that your entire survey research project is only as good as the sample, and that sample is only as good as the list from which it was drawn. If the list is biased—not representative of the population of interest—then your results will be biased as well. For example, suppose you use warranty cards to compile a list. Unfortunately, return rates for warranty cards are notoriously low—5% to 10% in many cases. Who knows how different the nonreturnees may be? Similarly, you may have a list of names of people who attended an industry conference. This could produce problems such as geographical bias (depending on conference location) or employer success bias (only companies healthy enough to have adequate travel funds sent people to the conference). *Know your list* is the rule, and be sure to keep its limits and shortcomings in mind as you analyze results.

STEP 4

Next you pretest the survey. I cannot overemphasize the importance of this step. In any substantial effort, you should plan on a small-scale administration to a few dozen members of the target population. After each person completes the survey, they are interviewed about possible misunderstandings, the meaning of their answers, and sources of confusion. A survey that may seem perfectly clear to a 38-year-old MBA-educated project manager immersed in the product category may be regarded very differently by a 24-year-old engineer who uses the product only on an occasional basis.

In real-world situations, you often will be tempted to skip the pretest because of time pressures. This is yet another example of how easy it is to do a bad survey. But remember: If the questions on the survey are confusing, if the list of answer categories is incomplete, or if the language is wrong, then it does not matter that you have a large, representative sample. Your results are that much more likely to approximate garbage. At the very least, ask your spouse and the spouses of teammates to look it over. Get *some* outside minds involved, even if it is only a half dozen.

STEP 5

The survey is administered. If it is a telephone survey, computer-assisted telephone interviewing probably will be used. The interviewer sits in front of a computer that flashes the questions on the screen and allows the interviewer to enter the answers directly into the tabulation and analysis software. The efficiency of such a procedure is obvious, and one of the reasons that telephone interviewing is preferred is that this automatic tabulation of answers speeds up the analysis and reporting cycle considerably. On the other hand, if it is a mail survey, then there will be an initial mailing followed by a postcard reminder and sometimes one or more follow-up mailings. One of the reasons mail surveys are less preferred is the amount of time consumed by this process combined with the low response rates (10%, 20%, 30%) that typically occur even with several reminders and follow-ups.

STEP 6

Next, the survey results are analyzed and reported. Typically, the basic form of the analysis will be a comprehensive breakout of the frequency of the answers to each question on the survey. For example, if the question was "Do you use your computer for any of the following applications?" the report might then include a chart showing the following:

Percentage Using Application
63% Word processing
35% Spreadsheets
29% Communications
28% Graphics
20% Games
37% Other

If the question had been "How satisfied are you with each aspect of your computer?" using a scale in which 10 equals *completely satisfied* and 1 equals *not satisfied at all,* the results might look similar to the following:

Average Performance Ratings
7.5 Performance
8.2 Color graphics
6.0 Expandability
5.7 Software availability
7.9 Reliability

Most reports also will include a number of cross-tabulations that combine answers to two or more questions. For instance, you might want to compare the applications typically used by owners of IBM PCs to those typically used by owners of Apple Macintoshes. Then you would see a chart something similar to the following:

Application	Used by IBM PC Owners (%) (n = 893)	Used by Apple Macintosh Owners (%) (n = 125)
Word processing	70	48
Spreadsheets	49	22
Communications	27	30
Graphics	12	58
Games	15	31
Other	29	78

A good report will include a variety of additional data. In an appendix or elsewhere, look for information on confidence intervals (i.e., the precision of the percentages or averages contained in the report). You need to know how many percentage points have to separate two estimates before you can trust that there is a real difference. Thus, in the first example above, with any decent-sized sample, we probably can conclude that word processing is a more common application than spreadsheets; but are spreadsheets really any more common than communication applications? There is no easy way to know unless the vendor has included the necessary information on confidence intervals. You must recognize that a survey gives only estimates of the true values in the total population, and any estimate is only that—a probable value. Do not fall into the trap of treating the numbers in a survey as an oracular pronouncement or a window onto truth.

Other data, whose presence should add to your comfort with the vendor and the survey, include information on response rate along with comparisons, to the extent possible, of how respondents differ from nonrespondents. If the response rate is low, your confidence in the results has to be lowered accordingly. For instance, you may have started out with a large, representative sample of technical support employees, but if only 10% of these people returned your survey, then your obtained sample is probably both small in number (making the results less precise) and systematically different from the population of interest—the total population of all technical support personnel in the market you serve. *If,* however, the list you used to obtain the sample contained some additional information beyond name and phone number—for instance, each support person's years of experience and whether he or she works in hardware or software support—*and* if you compared people who responded to the survey to people who did not, *then* you may be able to establish whether the obtained sample is biased on these two counts. If in fact the obtained sample of support personnel is similar to the initial sample in years of experience and in terms of the hardware-software split, then your confidence that the sample is representative goes back up, despite the low response rate.

On the other hand, if there is no information that allows a comparison between respondents and nonrespondents, then, as a rule of thumb, the lower the response rate, the less confidence you should have in the results (see Exhibit 6.1). Large percentage differences in the case of high response rates (i.e., a 62% to 38% split on an agree-disagree question when the response rate is 80%) are unlikely to vanish altogether even when there is substantial response bias. By contrast, the same majority of 62% agreement, but given a response rate of only 20%, will disappear if the nonrespondents happen to split 53% to 47% in the reverse direction. As a general rule of thumb, a small percentage difference (say, 55% to 45%) on an agree-disagree question will be virtually uninterpretable in the case of a low response rate. It could easily be the opposite of the true breakdown of responses in the population at large.

Exhibit 6.1 Why Low Response Rates Render Survey Results Moot

---

Assume: 1. An initial sample size of 1,000
         2. An agree-disagree item (i.e., "The Apple Macintosh is easier to use than the
            IBM PC") yielding an agreement rate of 62%

Case 1:   High response rate of 80%

          Thus, obtained sample = 800
          Raw totals   = 496 agree
                                   304 disagree

To upset this conclusion—that a majority perceives the Mac to be easier to use than the
IBM PC—would require a very different distribution of sentiment among nonrespondents
to the survey.

          Where nonrespondents   = 200
          Only if   3 agree (1.5%)
          And   197 disagree (98.5%)

will the conclusion be reversed (then 496 + 3 = 499 agree, and 304 + 197 = 501 disagree).
Although not impossible, such a marked response bias is highly improbable.

Case 2:   Low response rate of 20%

          Thus, obtained sample = 200
          Raw totals   = 124 agree
                                    76 disagree

Now to upset the conclusion—that a majority perceives the Mac to be easier to use than
the IBM PC—would require only a modest reversal in the distribution of sentiment
among nonrespondents to the survey.

          Where nonrespondents   = 800
          Only if   375 agree (47%)
          And   425 disagree (53%)

the conclusion will be reversed (then 124 + 375 = 499 agree, and 76 + 425 = 501 disagree). Such a response bias might occur for any number of reasons: if those actually responding are somewhat more likely to be Mac owners or are more likely to own older and
more primitive IBM PCs, and so forth.

Conducting the Survey Yourself

If you have another department within your firm conduct the survey
(your in-house market research staff, for instance), then this section does
not apply—that is not much different than retaining an outside specialist.
In this section, I am concerned with you—the generalist—doing the

survey yourself. Conducting your own survey is probably a *bad* idea if any of the following conditions hold true:

1. Major decisions will rest on the data obtained.
2. It is a lengthy survey designed to capture a great deal of information.
3. You want a large, high-quality sample to complete the survey.
4. You intend to conduct elaborate analyses of the data.

If the decision is that important, why would you not be willing to obtain the expertise of a skilled professional? Parts of survey research, especially conducting the interviews and tabulating and analyzing the replies, can be very labor- and time-intensive. Is it that you or your employees have idle time that you want to put to use? (Hah!) Moreover, writing a good questionnaire, defining a good sample, conducting the survey in an unbiased manner, and correctly analyzing the results are all specialized technical skills unlikely to be possessed by the typical product, project, or program manager.

By contrast, you probably *can* effectively conduct your own survey under the following circumstances:

1. The decision, although not unimportant, cannot justify a substantial expenditure.
2. You have a few straightforward questions and a couple of issues that you want clarified.
3. You would be content so long as the sample is not awful, you have a captive sample, or you can take a virtual census.
4. The goal of your analysis is to identify lopsided majorities or split opinions via simple tabulations.

These circumstances are not uncommon. Maybe you want to ask a few questions of your field salesforce, and their management has agreed to assist you. Maybe you have customers attending an event and you are curious about a couple of things. Likewise, you should have some kind of warranty card included with your product, and of course, this card should include a couple of questions. *If* you do not take any one instance of this kind of survey too seriously *and* you keep each such survey short and simple *and* you do these surveys as one part of your information gathering, then *yes* it makes sense to do these surveys and *yes* you can do them yourself.

You should, however, ask yourself several questions. First, will the survey really make any difference? What will you do with the data that you could not otherwise do? Any survey requires a chunk of your time—precious time of which you have too little. Second, how would your time be better spent: searching for high-quality secondary research or conducting a not great, not awful survey yourself? This has to be answered on a case-by-case basis. If no relevant or useful secondary data exist, then, of course, you may have no choice but to do your own survey. But it would be a shame if you labored mightily to produce an OK survey when in fact there existed some outstanding secondary research that you could have found if only you had gone to the trouble. Third, are you seeking a description or some understanding? If the latter, why not make a series of semistructured phone calls (a kind of customer visit), as opposed to firing off a written survey. A semistructured phone interview really is not a survey because it has so much flexibility. You are not calling to take a count but to get inside people's heads and gain a perspective. That is an interview, not a survey. In which case, you want a few starter questions, but you want the emphasis in the phone call to be on the follow-up questions that you formulate on the spot in response to what the person has said. As noted in the customer visit chapter (Chapter 4) and in contrast to survey research, you probably are better placed than an outside vendor to conduct an effective interview. So why not do what you do best?

Cost Factors

Sample size. Small samples of about 100 often can be surveyed for less than $10,000. Larger samples of 1,000 or more can drive the cost to well over $100,000.

Accessibility. If lists of these people are expensive, if the lists are bad so that many calls are wasted, if these people are hard to reach on the phone, if many refuse to participate, or if many terminate the interview prior to completion, then the cost goes up accordingly.

Survey length. Phone surveys that require 5 to 10 minutes to complete can be quite inexpensive. As length increases, the cost goes up even faster. Forty-five minutes for a phone interview and perhaps 12 pages for a mail questionnaire are probably the maximums.

Analysis. If you want many cross-tabulations, more sophisticated statistical analyses, or more elaborate reporting, then the cost increases. Analysis costs are, however, generally modest relative to the three factors named earlier.

Examples

Because surveys are such a familiar kind of research, this section will describe a range of applications rather than giving one or two specific case studies. Although the survey is an enormously flexible tool, the eight applications described next probably account for the bulk of the market research surveys conducted in a given year.

CUSTOMER SATISFACTION

In a customer satisfaction survey, a large and representative sample of a firm's customers will be telephoned and asked to rate the firm's performance in a variety of areas. These may include relatively specific actions (e.g., "Timely response to inquiries") and more general and intangible aspects (e.g., "Offers solutions that are at the cutting edge of the industry"). Customers also may be asked to indicate whether certain problems have occurred (e.g., "Has your system had any unscheduled downtime?"). Customers will give their ratings on 10-point scales or similar measures. The primary output of this survey will be numerical indexes that report, in both global and specific terms, how well the firm is doing. These satisfaction surveys will typically be repeated on a quarterly, semiannual, or annual basis so that trends can be discerned.

SEGMENTATION STUDIES

In a segmentation survey, a large and inclusive sample of customers for some product or service will be asked a variety of questions. For example, some years ago Levi Strauss conducted a survey to segment the market for men's clothing. Attitude questions (e.g., "Dressing right is a complete mystery to me"), shopping behaviors (e.g., "Do you prefer to shop on your own or with someone else?"), and usage data (e.g., "How many suits do you own?") were determined. The goal in a segmentation survey is to gather enough data that well-defined clusters of consumers with distinct buying preferences can be identified. In the Levi Strauss study, the "classic independent" segment emerged as the best target market for wool-blend clothing, as compared to some of the other segments (e.g., "mainstream traditionalists") for whom a different product (polyester suits) was more attractive. The primary goal of a segmentation survey is to provide a rich description of the differences between groups of consumers, along with linkages between these differences and behaviors of interest (heavy usage, product preference, etc.). Quite complex, multivariate statistical analyses can be performed to produce a pictorial representation of segment differences and preferences.

PRODUCT USAGE AND OWNERSHIP

In the case of innovative product categories, it is often of interest to know what kinds of people have adopted a product early in its life cycle, what they use it for, and what other products are used with it. For instance (this example was current in 1993 to 1994), what kinds of people have bought a CD-ROM drive for their personal computer? How many CD-ROMs have they bought for use with that drive? What categories of CD-ROMs have been bought (games, encyclopedia, maps, etc.)? Even mundane or mature products may benefit from a usage survey if years have passed since the last survey. A bank might survey its customers on which bank products are used (checking, savings, certificates of deposit, etc.), by whom, how heavily, and for what purpose. The primary goal in any product usage survey is to get more complete and detailed information on product users and nonusers so as to facilitate subsequent marketing, advertising, and product development efforts.

PURCHASE INTENTIONS

A purchase intentions survey examines how many of which kind of people intend to buy some product or service within the next 6 to 12 months. Sometimes these questions will be combined with a product usage survey. The primary goal in a product intentions survey is to get data useful for forecasting future sales.

BRAND IMAGE AND PERCEPTIONS

In a brand image survey, you try to understand how your brand is regarded in the marketplace (often in comparison with other brands). Most often, questions will take the form of rating scales ("On a scale of 1 to 5, how prestigious is this brand"), and the factors rated can range from "very tangible" to "very intangible" (e.g., *provides good value* versus *daring* or *mainstream*). Whereas a satisfaction survey is primarily evaluative—a kind of report card—a brand image survey is primarily descriptive—a profile or portrait. The goal in a brand image survey is typically either to more broadly diagnose problems (in the case of a brand that has lost ground in a market) or to diagnose strengths and weaknesses (often in preparation for a new advertising campaign).

TRACKING STUDIES

Advertisers use tracking studies to determine whether an ad campaign is having the desired effect. The typical procedure is to conduct a baseline survey prior to the launch of the ad campaign. The survey may measure brand awareness, brand image, knowledge of a brand's features and capabilities, usage type or frequency, or anything else that the advertising campaign is aimed at changing. At regular intervals following the launch of the campaign, this survey will be readministered to a new sample drawn so as to be comparable to the baseline sample. The primary goal of a tracking study is to determine whether the ad campaign is working and how well. If a tracking study is conducted apart from any ad campaign, then its purpose is probably trend monitoring, for instance, what people know about handheld computers or current beliefs about the effectiveness of their handwriting recognition capabilities. Also, some of the major advertising agencies conduct such surveys to monitor changes in lifestyles and values.

MEDIA USAGE

A media usage survey asks about magazines read, television programs watched, preferences in radio format, and so forth for some specified group of people (e.g., buyers of a certain product category, such as mutual funds). A media usage study will probably be conducted by the vendor firm or its ad agency to guide the allocation of ad spending toward the most efficient media vehicles. Thus, you may discover that a large number of networking engineers happen to read *Scientific American* magazine and that the ad rates in this magazine compare favorably with those of more obvious choices such as *PC Magazine*. Media spending is so substantial (Intel has spent hundreds of millions of dollars promoting its brand of processor chips, and Procter & Gamble spends over a billion dollars per year) that even a quite expensive media survey may quickly pay for itself if it leads to a marginally better allocation of media dollars.

READERSHIP STUDIES

A readership survey will be conducted by a magazine or other media vehicle to develop a profile of the people who read the magazine. Readers are the "product" that magazines sell to advertisers, who are their true customers (advertising dollars account for the bulk of magazine revenues). The readership questionnaire will ask demographic (e.g., age, occupation, and income), psychographic (e.g., attitudes, opinions, interests, hobbies, and lifestyle), and product usage questions. The primary goal is to describe the readership so as to facilitate efforts to market the magazine to advertisers. If you are a provider of instructional software aimed at children and if I can show you that my readers are very interested in education and child development, then I can hope to win some of your advertising dollars.

Strengths and Weaknesses

The great strength of survey research is its ability to deliver precise numerical estimates of the frequency and magnitude of some consumer response. Survey research tells us not that "many" customers are seeking some benefit but that 39% desire it, not that satisfaction has "decreased" but that satisfaction has dropped from 8.6 to 7.8 on a 10-point scale, and not that new computer owners "regularly" purchase software but that owners spend an average of $586 on software in the year following purchase. This strength is valuable because ultimately most businesses have to measure their success in precise numerical terms, that is, profit dollars, unit sales, market share percentage. In turn, survey research is most useful to businesses in situations in which precision matters a great deal—that is, in which small differences can be consequential. Thus, any percentage that ultimately concerns the potential size or growth of your market had better be precise. A few percentage points may translate to millions of dollars and may mean the difference between a market big enough to be worth pursuing or too small to consider entering. Similarly, precision is valuable when a high level of uncertainty would be intolerable. Thus, you could conduct lengthy visits with dozens of customers, hear all kinds of stories about your product, and still have no clear sense of whether the overall satisfaction of your customer base is increasing, staying level, or dropping. In any application that requires or resembles a scorecard, a forecast, or a comparison of magnitudes, the precision of survey research will be valuable.

A second strength of survey research lies in its superior objectivity—its capacity to break you free of biases. Every businessperson is continually creating and revising a mental map that describes his or her customers, competition, and markets, and all kinds of daily experiences feed into that map. Unfortunately, because virtually all businesses have to deal with markets that range in size from large to huge to gigantic to vast, the personal experience of each businessperson is necessarily limited and partial and thus biased to some unknown degree. Just as an automobile extends the legs and a telescope the eyes, a good survey extends personal inquiry. Your questions are put to a much larger number of people than you could personally interview, and this large number (in a good survey) represents that still larger population of customers that constitutes your market. Consequently, the survey can be thought of as a "question machine" that, as with all machines, functions to expand unaided human capacity.

In a sense, the amplification capacity of the survey or its ability to extend your individual effort actually functions to correct two kinds of biases—those due to personal *prejudice* as well as those due to personal *limitations*. That is, as individuals, we all have personal viewpoints that shape our perceptions. These viewpoints accommodate our idiosyncratic experiences—for instance, the angry customer we spoke to yesterday, the salespitch that works for us, the friendly customer that always takes our phone calls, and so forth. Unfortunately, no individual is "open" enough to keep in mind all the diverse components of an entire market. Of course, objectivity, as with precision, matters most when you face a close call and some evidence exists in favor of both options. Here the survey functions as the equivalent of a microscope, clarifying a difference too small to be reliably discriminated based on the personal experiences of you and your debating partners.

A third strength of survey research is that it allows you to apply a wealth of statistical techniques that can enhance the rigor and add to the depth of your knowledge. An enormous amount of academic research, developed over a period of 50 years or more, has been directed at developing tools for analyzing the kind of data that surveys produce. Although such narrowly focused and arcane academic research is sometimes the butt of jokes in practical business circles, let me suggest that statistical analysis is similar to the police—it is easy to have a dismissive attitude until the day your need is acute. How big is *big?* How precise is *precise?* How different is *different?* It is the purpose of statistical analysis to answer such questions, and when millions of dollars hang on getting the right answer, you may come to appreciate the many ways in which survey research lends itself to analysis in statistical terms.

Another strength of surveys is their capacity for illuminating and pinning down differences between groups. A large sample and a precise estimate enable you to do two things: (a) to determine whether a difference between groups really exists and (b) to more accurately describe the nature of any difference that does exist. Intergroup comparisons are typically important in segmentation analysis and in the assessment of strengths and weaknesses relative to the competition. For instance, suppose you find that your customers are, on average, working in larger facilities and concentrated in Sunbelt states, as compared to your competition. That knowledge will make your marketing efforts more effective. For another example, exactly how do people who prefer to put their savings in certificates of deposit differ from those who prefer to put their savings in money market mutual funds—in their education, income, source of savings, and geographical location? That knowledge can make your advertising appeals stronger. Again, small differences may have a major dollar impact on the efficiency of marketing and advertising efforts, and an effective survey research procedure may be the only way to uncover such differences.

Finally, surveys become especially powerful when they are repeated over time. There are a couple of reasons why repeating a survey at intervals is often money well spent. First, most markets are dynamic rather than static. Repeated surveys thus yield data on trends. Furthermore, actually possessing data from multiple past points in time probably provides a more accurate picture of the evolution of a market than asking customers to give a retrospective account of how things have changed over the past few years. Similarly, for forecasting purposes, you are better off projecting a trend from several data points than trying to take a single data point (i.e., the customer's self-forecast) and extrapolate from it.

From an alternative view, when a survey is repeated, many small biases that may bedevil a single administration cancel out. Thus, the estimate of brand awareness you took today may be off the mark because your sample is a biased subset of the population. But if you use the same questions and sampling procedure four to five times and the data show an upward trend, that trend is probably more reliable than the absolute value (i.e., 20% or 24%) that you estimated in any single administration.

Perhaps the most significant weakness of descriptive survey research is that it tends to tell you *what* but not *why.* You learn that customer satisfaction is down but you do not know why. You find out that a substantial percentage of your customers are interested in a piece of functionality but you do not learn what is driving that interest. Of course, this is not a problem if you combine the survey with more exploratory techniques such as focus groups or customer visits. It is a big problem if you expect to do only survey research for your market research effort.

A related but more subtle weakness is that typically a survey cannot reveal what you did not know you did not know. If you *do* know what it is that you do not know, then you can devise the questions and the answer categories needed to resolve that uncertainty. Surveys can readily answer a question such as, Which of these problems is most commonly experienced by our customers? Surveys are not very good, however, answering questions such as, What new and unexpected problems have begun to bother our customers? This is because surveys emphasize closed-ended questions in which the answer categories are prespecified rather than open-ended questions. In a word, surveys are a precision tool, not a discovery tool.

Another weakness of surveys is that they rely on self-report data. If the customer does not know something, cannot or will not verbalize that something, or cannot accurately describe that something, then a survey will not reveal it. Some examples of information you might wish to gain but that customers may be unable to self-report include the following:

(a) what they will do in the future, (b) what is the most important factor in their purchase decision (they can tell you what they think is important, but will this be reflected in their actual behavior?), (c) what other people in their organization think or do, (d) exactly how much time or money they spent on something, or (e) which parts of the user interface cause them to make errors. Just as the weaknesses of surveys with respect to explanation and discovery drive you to supplement surveys with focus groups and customer visits, so also the weaknesses associated with self-report data should drive you to supplement descriptive surveys with choice modeling, experimentation, and usability testing. In these alternatives, people *act* rather than, or in addition to, speaking, and analyses of these actions can reveal matters of which the customer is unaware or incapable of verbalizing.

A more subtle weakness of survey research is that most of the time, for most people, participation in a survey is intrinsically unrewarding. This is one reason why phone surveys are more commonly used in market research than mail surveys: It is harder to ignore or dismiss a phone call as opposed to a letter. Surveys are not fun. People participate out of inertia, out of a sense of obligation (recognizing that their information is probably useful), or to give voice (more likely in the case of aggrieved customers, which, of course, introduces a bias). In comparison to an interview, which is a person-to-person encounter and which offers potential rewards such as feeling understood, getting through to someone else, learning something, being stimulated to think, enjoying company, and so forth, ultimately participating in a survey means becoming grist for a statistical mill—an opportunity to be an instance of a population rather than a unique individual.

Two implications follow from this weakness. First, surveys tend to be most useful for getting broad but shallow data. You cannot ask hard, provocative, challenging questions because respondents will not play. You cannot do extensive follow-up on answers because you are not employing phone interviewers with that level of skill (and a mail questionnaire cannot have too many branching paths). Second, surveys have to be designed to minimize the costs of responding and to maximize the rewards (see Dillman, 1978, in the Suggested Reading section). In designing a survey, you have to drive toward brevity and ease of responding. Else, the cost goes way up and the quality goes down. If the survey is too taxing, so many people will discontinue that the representativeness of your obtained sample will be called into question.

Yet another weakness implicit in much of what has been said earlier is that surveys are only as good as the sample and the questions used. It would be fascinating to study how our society developed to the point in which ordinary college-educated people became prone to assume that surveys are clear glass windows onto the truth. The source of this delusion might be the respect paid to quantification or perhaps the rhetorical power of anything that sounds scientific. Howsoever, it is nothing short of appalling how credulous the average businessperson becomes when confronted with the average survey. *Do not fall into this trap!* Gazing on a four-color pie chart, the tendency is to say, "Wow—63% of the market wants the product to do this—let's build that functionality in!" A more accurate statement might be, "Sixty-three percent of the people we managed to get on the phone, whose names happened to be on the only list we could afford, and who stuck with us to this point in the survey answered the only question we knew to ask with an indifferent, 'Sure why not?' " Do not kid yourself that a survey yields truth. Think instead of surveys as yielding one more fallible data point, to be combined with other data that are fallible for different reasons, as input to a decision that ultimately remains your own but that is more likely to be successful because you gathered diverse kinds of data.

A final weakness of survey research applies mostly to business-to-business markets in which the characteristic purchase decision is made by a group rather than an individual. A survey of individuals is unlikely to address the group decision-making process effectively. Even if the total survey includes people holding various job roles, it probably was not designed to include the full set of job roles from each company included in the sample. This is one of the great advantages of on-site customer visits: You can meet with several decision makers at each firm you visit, alone or in groups.

Dos and Don'ts

Don't fall into the trap of assuming that a large sample size can overcome sample bias. True, small samples give unstable results, independent of whether there is systematic bias, but once the sample size is adequate, further doubling or tripling its size does not in any way reduce whatever systematic bias may be present. If your list contains an unusual percentage of chemists with PhDs, relative to the total population of chemists, then your obtained sample is going to be biased by this high education level, regardless of how big the sample is or how high the response rate might be. Consequently, there is no substitute for a good list or sampling procedure.

Do look at confidence intervals on all means and percentages contained in survey reports. Be sure to find out how big the difference between two numbers has to be before you can be confident that the difference is real.

Don't assume that you can draft a perfectly good questionnaire by yourself in a couple of hours. Insist on multiple drafts and input from coworkers. Do everything feasible to pretest the survey instrument with customers.

Do conduct focus groups or customer visits in preparation for surveys. Look to these exploratory procedures for information on what topics to include in the surveys, what language to use, what questions to ask, and what answer categories to use.

Don't assume that everything of interest is accessible to self-report, and don't assume self-reports are automatically trustworthy (pretesting helps here). For each question, ask yourself whether a customer who genuinely wants to help could actually report, remember, and articulate the answer to that question. Although customers will almost always *reply* to your questions, if the question makes no sense or requires too much effort, these replies may be essentially random.

Do prepare rough tables and table headings for all frequency counts and cross-tabulations you expect to produce in the analysis of the survey. The point of doing this is to see whether you actually have a use for or need of certain questions. The tendency in survey design is to ask a lot of questions in the hope that something interesting will emerge. This is a bad idea. When you are forced to rough out table headings in advance, you will find yourself asking in certain cases, "What's the point? What good will this do me?" Whenever you ask that, your next question should be, "Should I even bother with this particular item on the survey?" Often the answer is no.

Don't indulge idle curiosity. The longer the survey, the more it will cost and the more likely the obtained sample will prove to be unrepresentative because of excessive attrition. Every question in the survey should do a job that needs doing. If you cannot meet this standard—if your basic feeling is one of overwhelming ignorance or uncertainty and this is the factor driving you toward the kitchen sink approach to survey design—then you probably are not ready to conduct a survey. You need to do more secondary research or customer visits or focus groups.

Do ask managers to predict the results of key questions. Ask them what the major points of difference will be between two groups. Ask them to predict the approximate percentage of agreement and disagreement with certain opinion statements. The point of doing this is to make it impossible to say, after a survey has been done, "We already knew that," when in fact the results are a surprise. Documenting that survey research yielded a fresh perspective and corrected some misunderstandings is one of the ways that you establish the value of market research.

Do think of the survey as a social exchange between sponsor and respondent. Exchanges are facilitated when you find ways to minimize the perceived cost of the exchange and maximize the perceived benefits. In the case of surveys, you minimize the cost by keeping them short and making the questions as clear and easy to answer as possible. You maximize the benefits by making the questions relevant and of obvious importance—things a customer would want a vendor to know about or understand.

Suggested Reading

Converse, J. M., & Presser, S. (1986). *Survey questions: Handcrafting the standardized questionnaire.* Beverly Hills, CA: Sage

Sudman, S., & Bradburn, N. (1982). *Asking questions: A practical guide to questionnaire design.* San Francisco: Jossey-Bass.

These are two standard works from recognized authorities that focus on constructing a good questionnaire.

Dillman, D. A. (1978). *Mail and telephone surveys: The total design method.* New York: Wiley.

This is the best first book to read on survey research. It gives many practical suggestions and focuses on actions required to maximize response.

Dutka, A. (1994). *AMA handbook for customer satisfaction.* Lincolnwood, IL: NTC Business Books.

This is a comprehensive primer on how to measure customer satisfaction, with an emphasis on survey research applications.

Payne, S. L. (1951). *The art of asking questions.* Princeton, NJ: Princeton University Press.

This is a classic book on effective and ineffective ways to word questions.

Rossi, P. H., Wright, J. D., & Anderson, A. B. (1983). *Handbook of survey research.* New York: Academic Press.

The authors provide comprehensive coverage of topics associated with designing, conducting, and analyzing surveys.

Sudman, S. (1976). *Applied sampling.* New York: Academic Press.

>   Sudman addresses the issues involved in determining sample size and selection methods for surveys.

In addition to these, Sage (the publisher of this book) publishes dozens of titles on specific aspects of survey design and the statistical analyses commonly applied to surveys.

7

Choice Modeling

Any procedure that attempts to analyze how different factors combine to influence the choice of one product over another can be considered a kind of choice modeling. The underlying assumption is that any product or service offering can be conceptualized as a bundle of attributes. Each of these attributes may be more or less important to any particular buyer, and each attribute may be possessed to a greater or lesser degree by any particular product design. In general, attributes can be thought of as the components that make up the product's performance (e.g., how fast a computer is, how much memory it has, what software it can run, etc.) and also as points of difference that distinguish the offerings of various competitors (here more abstract attributes, such as reliability, availability of support, and vendor reputation, may come into play). All choice modeling procedures provide an estimate of the importance or the weight of each attribute in a buyer's purchase decision. Some procedures provide, in addition, a description of the optimal combination of attributes and attribute levels, whereas other procedures concentrate on comparing the strengths and weaknesses of existing competitive offerings and enabling "what-if" scenarios to be traced.

Choice modeling is one of the newest market research procedures and is generally the least familiar to a managerial audience. Because it has been a focus of academic research and development, a large number of approaches exist. To give you a sense of the range of options, we will look at two major kinds of choice modeling. *Conjoint analysis* is typically executed at a central site, whereas what I shall call the *direct weighting* approach typically is executed by means of a questionnaire. Each will be described in its own terms followed by a summary comparison.

Conjoint Analysis

STEP 1

Suppose you are designing a new 15-inch video monitor intended to be purchased as an upgrade to a personal computer. Experience suggests that the following attributes may be influential:

Price
Energy consumption
Dot pitch (how big each pixel that makes up the screen image is)
Speed of vertical refresh (how quickly the screen is redrawn)
Flatness of the screen
Bulk of the monitor
Position of brightness controls (front, side, back)

Note that most of these features are "nice to have," whereas the remainder are matters of taste. It will not do you much good to conduct customer visits to see whether these features matter to buyers; you already know that they do matter. What you do not know is precisely how important each attribute is. You also do not know which of these attributes is worth extra money, neither can you discern what the ideal combination of attribute levels and price point might be nor how consumers make trade-offs between attributes. A conjoint analysis study can potentially address all of these questions.

STEP 2

Given a set of design attributes to be studied, the next step is to decide how many levels of each attribute you will examine. The complexity of the study can quickly become unmanageable if too many levels of too many attributes are investigated. Even seven attributes, each with two levels, allows for 2^7 or 128 permutations of the video monitor design.

Two considerations have to be balanced when setting levels of the attributes. On the one hand, you want to investigate all the relevant levels of an attribute. If dot pitches of .25, .28, or .31 would either have very different implications for manufacturing costs or would have a significant impact on the usability or attractiveness of the monitor (i.e., the smaller the dot pitch, the more effective the reproduction of detailed images), then you have to include each of these levels in the design. On the other hand, if a dot pitch of .31 is really not an option (perhaps because respected magazines are on record that anything larger than .30 is unacceptable or because there is no difference in the manufacturing cost of .28 and .31 dot pitches), then it need not be studied. There is a limit to how many permutations you can reasonably ask a consumer to judge, and if you exceed this limit, the results may be meaningless. From yet another angle, if the attribute levels are too far apart (i.e., you study only dot pitches of .25 and .31), then the conjoint analysis will not help you as much as it might have when it comes to selecting the optimal design (i.e., you may find that .25 is strongly preferred, but you deny yourself the opportunity of discovering that the cheaper-to-manufacture dot pitch of .28 would have been equally satisfactory). Then again, if you use attribute levels that are too close (i.e., you look at dot pitches of .25, .26, .27, and .28), consumers may apply a "chunking" rule, categorizing .25 and .26 as "great detail" and .27 and .28 as "good detail," and proceeding from then on as if your conjoint design only had two levels of dot pitch. In that event, you doubled the complexity of your design for no gain in understanding.

In practice, the number of attributes and levels actually studied is determined partly by your budget and partly by a sorting out process wherein you determine what is really important to analyze and understand and what can be taken for granted. You may decide not to study dot pitch at all, reasoning that a pitch of .25 is objectively superior, not much more expensive to manufacture than larger pitches, and in any case, a strategic necessity given your business plan, which requires you to go head-to-head against competitor X, who has standardized on a dot pitch of .25. If you reason thus, you might choose to simplify your design by dropping this attribute altogether.

STEP 3

Next, you create cards that correspond to all the permutations that you want to test. A statistician or a specialist in conjoint analysis can help you devise a design that estimates all parameters of interest using the minimum number of permutations. Such a reduced design may include some absurd or unlikely designs, if they serve the purpose of efficient statistical estimation. However, the general rule is that if you would not consider selling a particular permutation, if a particular permutation is not feasible, or if you can predict the response to it, then you might leave it out, unless it is necessary for efficient statistical estimation. Application of this procedure may leave you with 20 or 30 permutations rather than the 128 that a full design having 7 attributes with two levels each would require. Specifically, you may end up with 9 different low-functionality, low-price designs, 6 moderate-functionality, moderate-price designs, and 5 high-functionality, high-price designs.

STEP 4

To continue our example, you now have perhaps 20 cards, each of which describes a possible video monitor design. Next, these cards will be administered to a good-sized sample (100+ people) drawn from the population of interest. As always, sample characteristics are crucial. The people who participate in the conjoint study must represent the population for whom the video monitor is being designed. It is *their* choice process that needs to be understood. No amount of powerful mathematics in the analysis stage can overcome the negative effects of a poor sample selection procedure.

STEP 5

Next, you determine what kind of rating or judgment procedure you want subjects to apply to the 20 monitor designs. Typically this will be a measure of preference—perhaps a 10-point scale in which 10 indicates a *very strong positive* reaction to the design and a 1 equals a *very strong negative* reaction. Other measures, such as a rank ordering of the designs, also are possible. Note in passing that it may be important to vary the order of presentation of designs across subjects; items presented at the beginning and end of any judgment task are subject to well-known biases, and these need to be controlled.

STEP 6

Finally, statistical analysis will be applied to determine utility weights for each attribute. In essence, the analysis considers the differences in expressed preferences and relates these back to variations in specific attributes. Was preference consistently higher whenever a design specified a smaller and less bulky monitor? If so, this attribute will have a high weight: It appears to be an important factor in choosing a monitor. Was there little or no difference in preference stemming from various levels of energy conservation? If so, the analysis will assign a low weight to this attribute. The analysis also will detect nonlinear preferences (i.e., situations in which preference is greatest for a middle level of some attribute). Part of the power of conjoint analysis is precisely that it allows you to estimate utility weights for each level of the attribute and not just the attribute as a whole. Perhaps a midsized monitor is preferred to either a very compact or very bulky monitor.

STEP 7

The analysis just described produces weights for each individual customer participating in the study. In that marketing strategies typically do not target individuals but either segments or entire markets, the final step in the conjoint study is to determine how the utility weights for individuals should be aggregated. If experience or inspection of the data suggests that preferences are relatively homogeneous, then one can simply lump all respondents together to determine average utility weights for each attribute.

Alternatively, there may be reason to believe that there are two, three, or four quite different segments with distinct preferences. A statistical procedure known as cluster analysis can then be applied to the initial conjoint results. Cluster analysis will separate respondents into groups based on the similarity of their utility weight profiles. Then, you can determine average utility weights for each attribute separately for each segment. This then indicates what the optimal product design would look like on a segment-by-segment basis. Note that if you anticipate performing such a segmentation analysis, then a larger sample size, perhaps closer to 500, will be required.

Direct Weighting of Attribute Importance

In conjoint analysis, products are presented as complete packages and the analysis decomposes the resulting judgments into utility weights for the individual attributes that were varied to create those descriptions. The customer never says directly, "Dot pitch is a big deal to me and it drives my decision"; rather, it is the analysis of choices actually made by the customer that yields this conclusion. An alternative form of choice modeling works in the other direction, beginning with direct ratings of attributes and going on to incorporate additional kinds of information, as described below. This direct weighting procedure typically examines actual existing products to infer the requirements for success for a new product. It is more flexible in the kinds of attributes that can be examined and not so tightly tied to concrete design features such as dot pitch.

STEP 1

Here the first step is to gather together the existing products that will make up the competitive set for your anticipated new product. For instance, perhaps the market for 21-inch computer monitors consists of eight offerings from five different manufacturers. Next, you must select a set of attributes on which each product offering will be rated. This is really the crucial step. If you leave out attributes that do play a role in the customer's decision of what to buy, then your resulting analysis will be faulty. If you incorporate attributes that are not relevant, then you dilute the cogency of the analysis and run the risk of misleading or imprecise answers. Although the second mistake is somewhat less threatening than the first, it is still important to minimize. Good exploratory research is crucial for identifying a complete and concise set of attributes. (This holds true for conjoint analysis also, but there, the vendors' interest in examining some particular design attribute also may be influential in the selection of what to include.)

STEP 2

Customers who participate in the study will rate each existing product offering on how effectively it delivers each particular attribute. Again, these attributes can be abstract or concrete—for example, product reliability, achievement of some specific level of performance, friendly support, availability of a wide range of options for customization. A 10-point scale might be used so that each product receives a score on each attribute that indicates the degree to which it delivers that attribute.

STEP 3

In addition, customers will rate the importance of each attribute according to their own buying decisions, again perhaps using a 10-point scale.

STEP 4

Some additional information will then be collected, with the specifics varying depending on which research firm is executing the study. This might include which products have actually been bought in the past and to what extent, or a rank order of preference or buying interest across the product offerings, for example.

STEP 5

A booklet or questionnaire is created to incorporate all of the measures just described. A good-sized sample, large enough and representative enough to allow results to be projected to the market, must then be recruited. Unlike the controlled experiments to be discussed in the next chapter, there actually is no minimum sample size for choice modeling: It is the representativeness criterion that is crucial here. In one case, a manufacturer of disk drive assemblies obtained ratings from all 128 buying firms that constituted the market for this product—thus ensuring representativeness by taking a census of the market.

STEP 6

Whether by mail or in person, the questionnaires that incorporate the ratings are completed and returned. Results may then be analyzed along several lines. First is a simple analysis of the perceived strengths and weaknesses of each product offering across the set of attributes. Second, you would examine your own product offering's performance on both the relatively important and the unimportant attributes. These analyses both indicate areas for improvement and determine what a new version of your product would need to deliver to be more successful than the existing offering. Yet another possible analysis would be to break respondents down into segments and compare perceptions and importance weights across segments. This analysis may indicate that your product's overall mediocre performance in the market is a composite of doing (a) an excellent job of delivering important attributes to one market segment, (b) a terrible job delivering one attribute that is highly important to a second segment, and (c) a mediocre job with respect to two attributes that are key for yet a third segment.

Beyond these analyses, research firms that specialize in this kind of study will typically have developed proprietary algorithms for adjusting the directly stated importance weights. This is where the ancillary information, such as the rank-ordered preference for all eight product offerings, gets used. A certain attribute may be rated only slightly more important, on average, than another, but good performance on this attribute seems to have a disproportionately larger effect on overall preference. This can be accounted for statistically.

Yet another alternative analysis is to investigate different combination rules across the attributes. The naive combination rule would be that buyers prefer the offering that has the highest weighted delivery score across the total set of attributes. This is referred to as a compensatory model because highly effective performance on an important attribute can compensate for moderately effective performance on several less important attributes. A more sophisticated combination rule might involve threshold effects; for example, perhaps improvements in the bulkiness of a monitor affect preference only once a certain level of reliability is obtained. Yet other combination rules might identify dependency effects between pairs of attributes—more effective performance on Attribute A only affects preference when performance also is high on Attribute B and vice versa—and also order effects—perhaps customers make their choice of monitor strictly on speed of vertical screen refresh, ignoring all other attributes unless product offerings are seen as equivalent on this count, whereupon the second most important attribute will be examined and so forth.

The payoff for all the elaborate analyses just described is the ability to run simulations. For example, what if you improved the perceived reliability of your monitors from fourth best to second best in this set of eight competitors? Given all the statistical adjustments described earlier, what would this enhanced reliability translate into regarding a projected increase in market share? The power of this kind of analysis is that you can estimate what kind of investment might be required to improve reliability to that degree and compare this level of investment with the enhanced profitability consequent on the larger market share to make a "go" or "no-go" decision about whether to improve the product in this way. In particular, note how understanding the true combination rules used by buyers might protect you from investing in expensive improvements that in fact will have no measurable impact on buyer preference (because of a failure to meet the threshold on other more crucial attributes).

COMMENTARY

Conjoint analysis and direct attribute weighting are used to solve somewhat different problems. Conjoint analysis works best with concrete *design* attributes, as in our video monitor example. It addresses the situation in which many possible combinations of features appear plausible or feasible and in which the goal is to determine the best or optimal combination. This makes sense when you have a wealth of design possibilities and you want to understand how customers trade off different combinations of functionality and price. You can think of it as a way to sort through and order a wealth of candidate new product designs subject to the provision that these designs concern specific models that can be characterized exactly by a particular combination of features.

Direct attribute weighting addresses a different situation in which the issues are more diffuse and also more inclusive. Brand information is typically not a factor in conjoint analysis (with the possible exception of brand name). Of course, in many business-to-business situations, products are purchased or not purchased for many reasons that have nothing to do with the presence or absence of some product feature. Whenever vendor reputation is important or when you want to understand how abstract perceptions involving factors such as reliability or timeliness of support come into play, then direct attribute weighting may be the more appropriate technique.

Direct attribute weighting addresses a situation in which you have an existing product and want to sort through possible improvements or alterations to find those that will have the most bang for the buck—that is, that are most likely to favorably influence buyers' decision processes. Direct attribute weighting, because of the what-if simulations that it makes possible, has an exploratory potential that is not present in the typical conjoint study.

Although direct attribute weighting may seem to have the wider applicability (almost any product aspect that can be expressed can function as an attribute for rating purposes), it does impose a subtle but important requirement: Buyers must be sufficiently familiar with several competitive offerings to be able to confidently rate them. It is possible to imagine, instead, markets in which most buyers are familiar only with the particular product that they use and cannot knowledgeably rate other products. Conjoint analysis does not suffer from this limitation because all products are treated as hypothetical offerings and customers make their judgments based solely on the stated features.

Finally, although conjoint analysis and direct attribute weighting as described here reflect two typical but distinct applications of the basic idea of choice modeling, they far from exhaust the possibilities. Other applications of the basic idea and diverse implementations of the two approaches described also exist, and more are being devised all the time.

In conclusion, it should be apparent to you that in this chapter I have skated quickly and very lightly over some deep mathematical and statistical waters. Choice modeling, whether performed by conjoint analysis or direct attribute weights or some hybrid procedure, is an intensive focus for "rocket science" in marketing research. The technical issues are both complex and controversial; some very bright people have worked for many years on different aspects of these problems and they have not always come to an agreement. Consequently, no answer can be given to such questions as to whether conjoint analysis is superior to the use of direct attribute weights or vice versa. Better to ask, Which of these procedures most closely addresses the specific issues that vex me today? More so than almost any other chapter in this book, the purpose of this discussion of choice modeling is not to show you how to do it but to get you thinking about whether it might be a good investment of your dollars to hire a specialist to work with you in designing a choice modeling study.

Strengths and Weaknesses

The great strength of choice modeling is the amount of complexity that these procedures can incorporate. This is most clearly seen if one contrasts the choice modeling procedures just described with an attempt to get at the same kind of information through a series of customer visits. Human beings simply are not that good at thoroughly explicating how they weight various factors in coming to a decision or what sort of combination rule they apply for integrating information. Nor are human beings (the data analysts in this case) all that good at integrating a mass of interview data to precisely delineate different choice models across several segments within a market. Customer visits *would* be quite effective at identifying attributes that matter and explaining why they matter and even at explaining why a customer might trade off in favor of one attribute rather than another. Customer visits also could help the data analyst glimpse the possibility that several different segments exist and what some key points of difference might be. But customer visits would be unlikely ever to provide the analytic precision that choice modeling so readily offers.

Another way to explain this key strength is that choice modeling goes beyond the customer's self-report. Rather, the consumer is given the opportunity to act within a carefully constructed situation and then powerful mathematical techniques are applied to the task of understanding those actions. This is most clearly seen in the case of conjoint analysis approaches, in which we analyze what the consumer does rather than what she or he says. Even the direct weighting approaches, which place greater reliance on self-report, nonetheless heavily structure this self-reporting and perform extensive transformations on it.

Choice modeling represents the acme of the application of modern statistical analysis to the solution of enduring business and marketing questions, such as how to design winning products and how to improve existing product offerings. It provides one of the clearest instances of the practical payoff of academically driven "research and development" within the marketing profession. Thirty years ago, it was practically impossible to do what anyone with a personal computer and a good statistical background readily can do today. Although choice modeling is hardly a panacea, it's difficult to imagine a substantial product design effort (absent the caveats and limiting conditions cited below) that would not benefit from some type of choice modeling initiative.

A related advantage of choice modeling procedures is the ability to deal with and sort through a large number of product design alternatives. This strength is most evident in contrast to the controlled experiments described in the next chapter. Most choice modeling techniques can either explicitly address a variety of design alternatives (as in conjoint analysis) or allow for simulation of the many possible alterations to an existing design.

Choice modeling also offers an interesting mix of confirmatory and exploratory opportunities. Although predominately a confirmatory technique in the sense that findings are constrained by your initial choices concerning what attributes to study, within those constraints it is possible to explore the probable outcome of making any number of changes in product design and positioning. A direct-weighting study done at the level of a product platform (i.e., the technological base from which several generations of specific product models will issue) may provide useful simulation opportunities for several years.

The most important weaknesses of choice modeling can be thought of as limits or constraints. Two are particularly crucial: (a) the sample of customers used and (b) the set of attributes examined. Just as a biased sample in a survey renders suspect or useless any number of precise percentage breakdowns, so also a biased sample in a conjoint analysis or direct weighting study could lead to seriously misleading results, in that you precisely describe the choice process of an idiosyncratic (and perhaps small) subsegment of the overall market. An even more fundamental limitation concerns the set of attributes chosen for study. Here the garbage in, garbage out rule applies: If crucial attributes are omitted, if the wrong levels are set, or if the attributes are poorly stated or misinterpreted by customers, then the results may be of little value.

Less crucial, but important to remember, is that choice modeling can take a long time and cost a large amount of money. (Although, similar to surveys, cost and time frame are actually highly variable; a straight-forward conjoint analysis on a single segment might not cost any more than a good focus group study.) Time and cost are less of a problem if, say, a direct weighting study is appropriately focused at the level of a platform technology that can be expected to endure for several years and spawn a stream of specific product configurations.

Finally, choice modeling can be difficult to implement for products purchased through a group decision process. More generally, it is necessary to assume that buyers process the information presented to them in the choice modeling exercise in the same way that they process that information in actual buying decisions. This assumption may not hold for buyers that have little experience with a product category, where market conditions are in flux or rapidly changing, or in the case of extremely new products whose implications may be difficult to grasp.

Dos and Don'ts

Don't try to put together the attributes for use in a choice modeling by huddling around a white board with your colleagues. Do go out into the field and use customer visits, focus groups, and other exploratory techniques to identify these attributes and ascertain the words customers use to represent them.

Don't assume that any convenience sample of potential customers will do. Strive to get the best possible sample to represent the population to which you want to appeal.

Don't be hasty in assuming that choice criteria and preference structures are basically the same for most buyers in the market. Do allow for the possibility of significant differences across segments.

Suggested Reading

Carmone, F. J., & Schaffer, C. M. (1995). [Review]. *Journal of Marketing Research, 32,* 113-120.

Carmone and Schaffer introduce and review conjoint software packages.

Green, P. E. (1984). Hybrid models for conjoint analysis: An expository review. *Journal of Marketing Research, 21,* 155-159.

>   Green describes ways of combining classic conjoint analysis with the direct-weighting approach.

Green, P. E., & Krieger, A. M. (1991). Segmenting markets with conjoint analysis. *Journal of Marketing, 55,* 20-31.

>   This work provides recommendations—illustrated with examples—for how to segment markets using conjoint analysis.

Green, P. E., & Srinivasan, V. (1990). Conjoint analysis in marketing: New developments with implications for research and practice. *Journal of Marketing, 54,* 3-19.

>   This article provides an overview of the variety of approaches to conjoint analysis now available.

Green, P. E., & Wind, Y. (1975). New ways to measure consumer judgments. *Harvard Business Review, 53,* 107-117.

>   This is perhaps the most accessible introduction to the technique, with numerous specific examples.

Wittink, D. R., & Cattin, P. (1989). Commercial use of conjoint analysis: An update. *Journal of Marketing, 53,* 91-96.

>   This work describes the kinds of conjoint analysis studies undertaken by practitioners during the 1980s.

Experimentation

Experiments can be conducted in the field or in some kind of laboratory—that is, an artificial situation constructed by the researcher. The essence of any experiment is the attempt to arrange conditions in such a way that one can infer causality from the results. In practice, this means creating conditions or treatments that differ in one precise respect and then measuring some outcome of interest across the different conditions or treatments. Differences in that outcome (how many people buy, how many people prefer) can then be attributed unambiguously to the difference between the treatments. In a word, one shows that the treatment *caused* the outcome.

Experimentation should be considered whenever you want to compare a small number of alternatives to select the best. Three common examples would be selecting the best advertisement from among a pool of several, selecting the optimal price point, or selecting the best from among several product designs. To conduct an experiment in any of these cases, you would arrange for equivalent groups of customers to be exposed to the ads, prices, or product designs being tested. The ideal way to do this would be by randomly assigning people to the various conditions. When random assignment is not possible, some kind of matching strategy can be employed. For instance, two sets of cities can provide the test sites, with the cities making up each set selected to be as similar as possible as to their size of population, age and ethnicity of residents, per capita income, and so forth. It has to be emphasized that an experiment is only as good as its degree of control; if the two groups being compared are not really equivalent or if the treatments differ in several respects, some of them unintended (perhaps due to problems of execution or implementation), then it will no longer be possible to say whether the key treatment difference caused the difference in outcomes or one of those other miscellaneous differences was in fact the cause.

Because experiments are among the less familiar forms of market research and because many of the details of implementing an experiment will be carried out by specialists, it seems more useful to give extended examples rather than walking you through the procedural details as has been done in previous chapters. The examples will address the three typical applications for experimentation—selecting among advertisements, price points, or product designs.

Crafting Direct Mail Appeals

This is one type of experiment that virtually any business that uses direct mail appeals, however large or small, can conduct. All you need is a supply of potential customers who number in the hundreds or more. First, recognize that any direct mail appeal is made up of several components, for each of which you can imagine various alternatives: for example, what you say on the outside of the envelope, what kind of headline opens the letter, and the details of the discount or other incentive. Imagine that you are torn between using one of the following two headlines in your next direct mail effort:

1. For a limited time you can steal this circuit board.
2. Now get the circuit board rated #1 in reliability.

These represent, respectively, a low price versus a high-quality lead-in. The remainder of each version of the letter will be identical. Assume further that the purpose of the campaign is to promote an inventory clearance sale prior to a model changeover.

To conduct an experiment to determine which of these appeals is going to produce a greater customer response, you might do the following.

1. Select two samples of 150 or more customers from the mailing lists you intend to use. A statistician can help you compute the exact sample size you need (larger samples allow you to detect even small differences in the relative effectiveness of the two appeals, but larger samples also cost more). Next, you would use an unbiased technique to assign names to the two samples; for instance, select every 10th name from the mailing list you intend to use for the campaign, with the first name selected assigned to Treatment 1, the second to Treatment 2, the third to Treatment 1, and so forth. Note how this procedure is more likely to produce equivalent groups than, say, assigning everyone whose last name begins with A to Treatment 1 and everyone whose last name begins with M to Treatment 2. It is easy to see how differences in the ethnic backgrounds of the A and M groups might interfere with the comparison of treatments by introducing extraneous differences that have nothing to do with the effectiveness or lack thereof of the two headlines under study.

2. Create and print two alternative versions of the mailing you intend to send out. Make sure that everything about the two mailings is identical except for the different lead-in: same envelope, mailed the same day from the same post office, and so forth.

3. Provide a code so that you can determine the treatment group to which each responding customer had been assigned. This might be a different extension number if response is by telephone, a code number if the response is by post card, and so forth. Most important, be sure that staff who will process these replies understand that an experiment is under way and that these codes must be carefully tracked.

4. After some reasonable interval, tally the responses to the two versions. Perhaps 12 of 150 customers responded to the high-quality appeal, whereas only 5 of 150 customers responded to the low-price appeal. A statistical test can then determine whether this difference, given the sample size, is big enough to be trustworthy.

5. Next, implement the strongest treatment on a large scale for the campaign itself, secure in the knowledge that you are promoting your sale using the most effective headline from among those considered.

COMMENTARY

The example just given represents a field experiment: real customers, acting in the course of normal business and unaware that they were part of an experiment, had the opportunity to give or withhold a real response—to buy or not to buy. Note the role of statistical analysis in determining sample size and in assessing whether differences in response were large enough to be meaningful. Note, finally, the assumption that the world does not change between the time when the experiment was conducted and the time when the actual direct mail campaign is implemented. This assumption is necessary to infer that the treatment that worked best in the experiment also will be the treatment that works best in the campaign. If, in the meantime, a key competitor has made some noteworthy announcement, then the world has changed and your experiment may or may not be predictive of the world today.

In our example, the experiment, assuming it was successfully conducted (i.e., all extraneous differences controlled for), establishes that the "rated #1" headline was more effective than the "steal" headline. Does the experiment then show that quality appeals are generally more effective than low-price appeals in this market? No. The experiment establishes only that *this* particular headline did better than this *other* particular headline. Only if we did many such experiments, using many varieties of low-price and low-quality headlines and getting similar results each time, might we tentatively infer that low-price appeals in general are less effective in this market. This one experiment alone cannot establish that generality. You also should recognize that the experiment in no way establishes that the "rated #1" headline is the *best possible* headline to use; it shows only that this headline is better than the one it was tested against. The point is that experimentation, as a confirmatory technique, logically comes late in the decision process and should be preceded by an earlier, more generative stage in which possible direct mail appeals are identified and explored so that the appeals finally submitted to an experimental test are known to be credible and viable. Otherwise, you may be expending a great deal of effort merely to identify the lesser of two evils.

Much more elaborate field experiments can be conducted with magazine and even television advertisements. All that is necessary is the delivery of different advertising treatments to equivalent groups and a means of measuring outcomes. Thus, split-cable and single-source data have become available in the past decade. In split cable, a cable television system in a geographically isolated market has been wired so that half the viewers can receive one advertisement, while a different advertisement is shown to the other half. Single-source data add to this a panel of several thousand consumers in that market. These people bring a magnetic card when they go shopping for groceries. It is handed to the cashier so that the optical scanner at the checkout records under their name every product that they buy. Because we know which consumers received which version of the advertisement, it is possible to determine empirically which version of the ad was more successful in stimulating purchase. For an example of a magazine advertising experiment in a business-to-business context, see Maples and Wolfsberg (1987) in the Suggested Reading section.

Selecting the Optimal Price

Pricing is a topic that is virtually impossible to research in a customer visit or other interview. If asked, "How much would you be willing to pay for this?" expect the rational customer to lie and give a low-ball answer. Similarly, the absurdity of asking a customer, "Would you prefer to pay $5,000 or pay $6,000 for this system?" should be readily apparent. Experimentation offers one solution to this dilemma; choice modeling offers another, as described earlier.

The key to conducting a price experiment is to create different conditions whose *only* difference is a difference in price. Marketers of consumer packaged goods often are able to conduct field experiments to achieve this goal. A new snack product might be introduced in three sets of two cities and only in those cities. The three sets are selected to be as equivalent as possible and the product is introduced at three different prices: $2.59, $2.89, and $3.19, say. All other aspects of the marketing effort (advertisements, coupons, personal sales) are held constant across the three conditions and sales are then tracked over time. Although one would, of course, expect more snack food to be sold at the $2.59 price, the issue is *how much more*. If the cost of goods is $1.99 so that a gross profit of 60 cents is earned per package at the $2.59 price, then the low-priced, $2.59 package must sell at twice the level of the high-priced, $3.19 package (in which $1.20 per package is earned) to yield the same total amount of profit. If the experiment shows that the $2.59 package has sales volume only 50% higher than the $3.19 package, then a business would probably be better off with the higher price. Note how in this example the precision of estimate supplied by experimentation is part of its attraction.

Business-to-business and technology marketers often are not able to conduct a field experiment as just described. Their market may be national or global, or product introductions may be so closely followed by a trade press that regional isolation cannot be obtained. Moreover, because products may be very expensive, hence dependent on personal selling, it may not be possible to set up equivalent treatment conditions. (Who would believe that the 10 salespeople given the product to sell at $59,000 are behaving in a manner essentially equivalent to the 10 given it to sell at $69,000 and the 10 given it to sell at $79,000?) Plus, product life cycles may be so compressed that an in-market test simply is not feasible. As a result, laboratory experiments, in which the situation is to some extent artificial, have to be constructed to run price experiments in the typical business-to-business or technology situation. The following is an example of how you might proceed.

1. Construct an experimental booklet in which each page gives a brief description of a competitive product. The booklet as a whole should describe all the products that might be considered as alternatives to your product, with one page in the booklet describing your own product. The descriptions should indicate key features, *including price*, in a neutral, factual way. The goal is to provide the kind of information that a real customer making a real purchase decision would gather and use.

2. Select a response measure. For instance, respondents might indicate their degree of buying interest for each alternative or how they would allocate a fixed sum of money toward purchases among these products. Various measures can be used in this connection; the important thing is that the measure provides some analogue of a real buying decision. This

is why you have to provide a good description of each product—to make responses on the buying interest measure as meaningful as possible.

3. Create different versions of the booklet by varying the price. In one example, a manufacturer of handheld test meters wished to investigate possible prices of $89, $109, and $139, requiring three different versions of the booklet.

4. Recruit a sample of potential customers to participate in the experiment. This sample must be drawn in as representative a fashion as possible from among the population of potential customers. Otherwise, their responses are useless for determining the best price. Moreover, members of the sample must be randomly assigned to the treatment groups. If administration is to be by mail, it also makes sense to see whether the actual respondents to the three treatments remain equivalent. If one type of buyer has tended to drop out of one treatment condition, for whatever reason, confidence in the results is correspondingly reduced.

5. Administer the experimental booklet. Quite often this will be by mail due to considerations of cost and a desire for geographical dispersion. It also could be done in person at a central site(s).

6. Analyze the results. In this price example, one would examine differences in the projected market share for the product at each price (i.e., the percentage of respondents who indicate an interest or who allocate dollars to the product, relative to response to the competitive offerings). To understand the results, extrapolate from the projected market shares for the product at each price point to what unit volume would be at that level of market share. For example, the $89 price might yield a projected market share of 14% corresponding to a unit volume of 76,000 meters. Next, construct an income statement for each price point. This will indicate the most profitable price. Thus, the $109 price may yield a market share of only 12%, but this smaller share, combined with the higher margin per meter, nevertheless yields a larger total profit.

What is accomplished by means of this experiment is an investigation of the price elasticity of demand—that is, how do changes in price affect demand for the product. Of course, demand probably will be lower at the $109 price than at the $89 price; again, the question is exactly how much lower? You might find that essentially no one is interested in the product at the highest price tested. In other words, demand is very elastic so that interest drops off rapidly as the price goes up a little. The experiment in that case has averted disaster. Or (as actually happened in the case of the handheld test meter example), you might find that projected market share was almost as great at the $139 price as at the $89 price, with, of course, much higher total profit (which is only to say that demand proved to be quite inelastic). In this case, the experiment would save you from leaving a great deal of money on the table through overly timid pricing.

COMMENTARY

Whereas a direct mail experiment can be conducted by almost any businessperson with a little help from a statistician, you can readily understand why, in a semilaboratory experiment such as just described, you might want to retain an outside specialist. Finding and recruiting the sample and ensuring as high a return rate as possible are nontrivial skills. Selecting the best response measure takes some expertise as well. In fact, a firm with a long track record can probably provide the additional service of comparing your test results with norms accumulated over years of experience.

Note that your level of confidence in the results of a laboratory experiment will almost always be lower than in the case of a field experiment. In the direct mail example, the experiment provided an exact replica of the intended campaign, except that it occurred at a different point in time with a subset of the market. A much larger gulf has to be crossed in the case of inferences from a laboratory experiment. You have to assume that (a) the people in the sample do represent the population of potential customers, (b) their situation of receiving a booklet and perusing it does capture the essentials of what goes on during an actual purchase, and (c) the response given in the booklet does represent what they would actually do in the marketplace if confronted with these products at these prices. By contrast, in the direct mail case, the sample can easily be made representative in that it is drawn from the same list, the experimental stimulus is identical with the real ad to be used, and the experimental response is identical to the actual response—purchase. Nonetheless, when field experiments are not possible, laboratory experiments may still be far superior to relying on your gut feeling—particularly when your gut feeling does not agree with the gut feeling of a respected and influential colleague.

Selecting a Product Design

Suppose that you have two or three product concepts that have emerged from a lengthy development process. Each version emphasizes some kinds of functionality over others or delivers better performance in some applications rather than others. Each version has its proponents or partisans among development staff, and each version can be characterized as responsive to customer input obtained through earlier qualitative and exploratory research. In such a situation, you would have two related questions: (a) Which one is best? and (b) What is the sales potential of that best alternative? (a forecasting question). The second question is important because you might not want to introduce even the best of the three alternatives unless you were confident of achieving a certain sales level or a certain degree of penetration into a specific competitor's market share.

Generally speaking, the same approach described under the pricing example can be used to select among these product designs. Whereas in the pricing example you would hold your product description constant and vary the price across conditions, in this product development example you would vary your product description across three conditions while you would *probably* hold price constant. Of course, if your intent was to charge a higher price for one of the product designs to reflect its presumed delivery of greater functionality, then the price would vary along with the description of functionality. Note, however, that the experimental results can address only the differences between the complete product descriptions as presented. If these descriptions differ in more than one respect, the experiment in no way tells you *which* respect caused the outcomes observed. Suppose that you find that the high-functionality, high-price product design yields exactly the same level of customer preference as the medium-functionality, medium-price design. At least two explanations, which unfortunately have very different managerial implications, would then be viable: (a) The extra functionality had no perceived value, and the price difference was too small to have an effect on preference, and (b) the extra functionality did stimulate greater preference, which was exactly balanced by the preference-retarding effect of the higher price.

It has to be emphasized that the cleanest and most certain inferences can be drawn when the product designs being tested differ in exactly one respect, such as the presence or absence of a specific feature or functionality. If both product design and price are an issue, then it may be best to either run two successive experiments—one to select a design and a second to determine price—or to run a more complex experiment in which both product design and price are systematically varied—that is, an experiment with six conditions composed of three product designs each at two price levels. Alternatively, choice modeling may provide a better approach than an experiment. The product design experiment can be conducted by mail, as in the price example, or, at the extreme, at a central site using actual working prototypes and examples of competitor products.

COMMENTARY

It may be instructive to compare the merits of a controlled experiment to choice modeling via conjoint analysis in selecting the optimal product design. The most important limitation of controlled experiments is that you are restricted to testing a very small number of alternatives. You also are limited to an overall thumbs-up or thumbs-down on the alternative as described. In conjoint studies, you can examine a large number of permutations and combinations. Conjoint analysis is also more analytic: It estimates the contribution of each product component to overall preference rather than simply rendering an overall judgment. Conversely, an advantage of controlled experiments is the somewhat greater realism of seeing product descriptions embedded in a context of descriptions of actual competitive products. Similarly, product descriptions often can be lengthier and more representative of the sales literature that buyers will actually encounter, unlike conjoint analysis, in which sparse descriptions are preferred to foreground the differences in the level and type of product attribute that differentiate the design permutations under study. The final advantage of experimentation is the potential for forecasting. The obtained share of preference for a design in the context of competitor product descriptions is more readily generalized to real market conditions than the more abstract preference judgments obtained in conjoint analysis.

Strengths and Weaknesses

Experimentation has one crucial advantage that is so simple and straightforward that it can easily be overlooked or underplayed: Experiments yield causal knowledge. Experiments predict what will happen if you do X or choose Y. Although strictly speaking, even experiments do not offer the kind of "proof" available in mathematics, experiments provide perhaps the most compelling kind of evidence available from any kind of market research, with field experiments being particularly strong on this count. In short, experiments represent a straightforward application of the scientific method to marketing decisions.

Experimentation has two subsidiary strengths. First, the structure of an experiment corresponds to one of the knottiest problems faced in business decision making: selecting the best from among several attractive alternatives. This is the kind of decision that, in the absence of experimental evidence, is particularly prone to politicking, to agonizing uncertainty, or to a despairing flip of the coin. In their place, experiments offer empirical evidence for distinguishing between good, better, and best. The second strength of experiments is the opportunity they afford for forecasting sales, profit, and market share (again, this is most true of field experiments). The direct mail experiment described earlier provides a forecast or prediction of what the return rate and hence the profitability will be for the campaign itself. The pricing experiment similarly provides a prediction of what kind of market share and competitive penetration one can achieve at a specific price point, whereas the product design experiment provides the same kind of forecast for a particular configuration of functionality. These forecasts can be used to construct pro forma income statements for the advertising, pricing, or product decision, and these in turn can be compared to corporate standards or expectations to make a "go" or "no-go" decision (i.e., even the best of the product designs tested may produce too little revenue or profit to be worthwhile). Other forecasting methods (e.g., extrapolation from historical data or expert opinion) are much more inferential and subject to greater uncertainty.

Experimentation is not without weaknesses. These mostly take the form of limits or boundary cases beyond which experimentation simply may not be feasible. For example, suppose there are only 89 buyers worldwide for your product category. In this case, you probably cannot construct two experimental groups large enough to provide statistically valid inferences and sufficiently isolated to be free of reactivity (which occurs when buyers in separate groups discover that an experiment is going on and compare notes). In general, experiments work best when there is a large population from which to sample respondents. A second limit concerns products bought by committees or groups. It obviously does you little good if an experiment haphazardly samples fragments of these buying groups. You either must pick one kind of participant and confine the experiment to them with consequent limits on your understanding or find a way to get groups to participate in the experiment, which dramatically increases the costs and complexity.

More generally, experiments decide only between options that you input. Experiments do not generate fresh options, and they do not indicate the optimal possible alternative—they only select the best alternative from among those specified. This is not a problem when experiments are used correctly as the culmination of a program of research, but it can present difficulties if you rush prematurely into an experiment without adequate preparation. A related problem is that one can select only among quite a small number of alternatives. Choice modeling is a better route to go if you want to look at a large number of possibilities. Finally, experiments can take a long time to conduct and can potentially tip off competitors.

Dos and Don'ts

Don't be overhasty in arranging to do an experiment. You really have to know quite a lot about customers and the market before an experiment can be valuable. If conducted prematurely, you risk getting wonderfully precise answers to the wrong question.

Don't let fear of costs prevent you from doing an experiment when appropriate. A laboratory experiment such as the price and product design examples described earlier may cost no more than a focus group study and considerably less than large sample survey research.

Do obsess about getting the details exactly right in your experimental design. The test groups have to be made as equivalent as possible, and the test stimuli have to differ in precisely those respects, and only those respects, under investigation.

Don't be afraid to be a pioneer. Experimentation is one of several areas of market research in which business-to-business and technology firms tend to lag far behind consumer goods firms with respect to best practice.

Don't expect brilliant new ideas or stunning insights to emerge from experiments. Experimentation does one narrow thing extremely well: It reduces uncertainty about whether a specific message, price change, or product design will have the desired effect. Experimentation is confirmatory market research par excellence; it is not a discovery tool.

Do consider whether the very best experiment might be to just put the product out on the market. Sometimes the expense and difficulty of experimentation, along with the ineradicable uncertainty expected to remain, make it better to go straight to market and let the initial sales results guide future product revision. This is simply another application of the investment mind-set in Chapter 1—if experiments aren't going to pay their way, don't do them.

Suggested Reading

Lodish, L., Abraham, M., Kalmenson, S., Livelsberger, J., Lubetkin, B., Richardson, B., & Stevens, M. E. (1995). How T.V. advertising works: A meta-analysis of 389 real world split-cable T.V. advertising experiments. *Journal of Marketing Research, 32,* 125-139.

> This is a fascinating examination of general principles revealed by split-cable advertising experiments. These authors also provide a guide to other studies in this vein.

Maples, M. J., & Wolfsberg, R. L. (1987). The bottom line: Does industrial advertising sell? *Journal of Advertising Research, 27,* 4-16.

> This article describes a field experiment using magazine ads in business-to-business markets.

Sawyer, A. G., Worthing, P. M., & Sendak, P. E. (1979). The role of laboratory experiments to test marketing strategies. *Journal of Marketing, 43,* 60-67.

> This work provides a good introduction, using an extended example, to issues involved in using laboratory experiments to test marketing strategies.

Shocker, A. D., & Hall, W. G. (1986). Pretest market models: A critical evaluation. *Journal of Product Innovation Management, 3,* 86-107.

> The authors discuss how the data from experiments can be transformed to produce reliable forecasts of market share and evaluate the strengths and weaknesses of various approaches to this problem.

Sternthal, B., Tybout, A. M., & Calder, B. J. (1994). Experimental design: Generalization and theoretical explanation. In R. P. Bagozzi (Ed.), *Principles of marketing research* (pp. 195-220). New York: Basil Blackwell.

> This chapter provides a state-of-the-art discussion of conceptual issues that arise in the design of different kinds of experiments.

PART III

9

New Market
Research Techniques

■ The marketing research discipline remains dynamic, and new techniques continue to evolve. You can expect academics to pioneer new statistical methodologies and practitioners and consultants to assemble new procedures to address old questions. This chapter will touch briefly on three emerging techniques of particular interest in business-to-business and technology markets. *Usability testing* focuses on the interaction between user and product. *Contextual inquiry* emphasizes observation of users in their natural context. *Computer simulations* provide a new approach to experimentation.

Usability Testing

In a usability test, a sample of potential users interacts with a product or prototype under carefully controlled conditions. For example, you may be working on a new piece of software that you have designed to accomplish certain tasks, to meet requirements identified in earlier market research, and to be an improvement on earlier solutions. Implicit in your design is a mental model of how users will interact with your software. Usability studies provide a way to test whether your model is correct by observing what happens when users actually attempt to use your product. Where do they make mistakes, and what kind of mistakes occur? Where do they get confused or become hesitant?

Usability testing is unique relative to traditional marketing research techniques in that it examines the *interaction* between product and user. Other market research techniques typically describe a stance, event, act, or recollection. In surveys, customers agree or disagree with statements about the product (i.e., take a stance) or state frequency or amounts (with respect to events). In choice modeling and controlled experiments, customers make choices (i.e., acts) that are analyzed. In customer visits and focus groups, customers tell stories (i.e., provide recollections). None of these approaches readily addresses the interaction between user and product in a way that facilitates redesign or the correction of design errors. People are notoriously poor at the task of accurately describing step-by-step what they do in a certain situation. Such self-knowledge is tacit and inaccessible. It is far more effective to provide an environment in which people perform some action and then to closely observe that behavior. Consequently, whereas other techniques easily can reveal that something is wrong with a product's design (i.e., customers rate it poorly or do not choose it), usability testing has the advantage when it comes to diagnosing exactly why a product is rated hard to use and also when it comes to evaluating several potential solutions to usage problems.

To see the relevance of usability testing in business-to-business and technology markets, consider for a moment a product that probably has *not* been the recipient of much in the way of standard usability testing: the ordinary toaster. It is simple to operate a toaster. There is a lever or an on-switch that serves to depress the bread into the heating area, along with some kind of darkness control. Moreover, the design has not changed much during most of our lifetimes. Of course, even this simple, mature technology is not without design issues: how much resistance the lever should offer, whether the darkness control should be a dial or a toggle, or how the two controls should be placed relative to one another, for example. Nonetheless, the toaster scarcely demands the full panoply of laboratory testing equipment associated with formal usability testing.

Compare now the microwave oven. Two contrasts immediately emerge. First, this is *novel* technology: If you are over 20, you did not grow up using one. Second, the microwave oven is capable of many more operations than a toaster—it is a complex machine. Third, these operations lie latent or hidden behind a control panel—there is no equivalent of a lever sitting at the top of a vertical slot, calling out to be pushed down. Rather, the microwave oven will not operate until a command sequence is entered. One must know the "code" to release its powers.

Generalizing from this contrast, one may say that usability testing will generally be rewarding in the case of any novel, complex product. Two corollaries can be added: that any software-driven product is by definition complex and that novelty and complexity compound one another's effects. In all such cases, one needs to study more than customers' stories, reactions, or choices—one needs to examine their interaction with the product in the context of completing some task(s). It helps to remember that modern usability testing grew out of early human factors research that focused, among other things, on the design of instrument panels for fighter planes.

Usability testing, however, is not limited to products per se. Any novel, complex activity can be submitted to usability testing. Two examples of particular relevance are documentation and shipping or installation procedures. Documentation is intended to help users perform new or unfamiliar tasks—but does it? It would be straightforward to recruit a sample of new or novice users, situate them in the testing area with a working prototype of the product and all documentation, and then ask them to perform a number of tasks, consulting the documentation as necessary. Where do people get confused, hung up? Where do they frown in puzzlement? Similarly, technology products—a computer workstation, for example—often arrive in the form of half a dozen carefully packed boxes containing twice as many booklets or manuals. Someone has to convert these boxed components into an installed, functioning product. For a usability test, one could recruit such installers, place them in a room, and instruct them to "set it up." How easy is it, really? In both these examples, it is processes rather than products per se that are the focus. Usability testing easily accommodates such extensions.

PROCEDURE

1. Find or create a laboratory. Many large companies have set up their own usability test areas; outside suppliers also can be found. These usability labs are designed to facilitate observation and measurement and generally will provide (a) one-way glass for unobtrusive observation, (b) videocameras to record both actions and facial expressions, (c) capture devices to record the sequence of keystrokes, and (d) some kind of precise clock synchronized with all other equipment. The purpose of using a laboratory is to ensure that each user in the study confronts the same testing conditions.

2. Determine your tasks. You cannot just tell people to "please interact with this product." Instead, you need to decide on a set of tasks that the user will attempt. These tasks should be grounded in the primary applications for the product or should relate to troubling or unresolved design issues, as identified by prior market research.

3. Recruit users. As always, the sample of people studied should reflect the population of interest. Although not uncommon, it is dangerous to assume that human usability responses are invariable and that any convenient set of humans will do. Particularly troublesome is the exclusive reliance on company employees—software companies tend to contain a high proportion of people who are very comfortable with computers and who may not represent actual users of the product very well.

4. Evaluate your results. Delays, errors, or unexpected responses can all be used to diagnose problems with the design. In this regard, perhaps nowhere else in market research is it so important to have the product designers intimately involved in the evaluation of results. The user interface being tested was designed the way it was for reasons fully known only to the designers themselves. They can best evaluate the implications for redesign, advised and guided, of course, by usability professionals who can bring the experience of many other tests to bear.

STRENGTHS AND WEAKNESSES

As discussed, the key strength of usability testing is its focus on the product in use and the user in interaction with the product. Moreover, usability testing represents an application of laboratory methods to these issues. In the old days, some technology firms relied on focus groups to accomplish a kind of usability testing. The lack of a consistent protocol for interaction with the prototypes, the probability of group influence, and the fragmentary character of individual participants' interaction with the prototype, however, all make focus groups decisively inferior to a laboratory approach to usability testing.

A second important strength is the reliance on observation. Just as choice modeling and controlled experiments obtain actions from customers rather than self-reports of mental states, so also usability testing obtains samples of behavior. Moreover, most usability tests also provide opportunities for users to vocalize what they are doing or to be debriefed after the conclusion of the test, thus providing a rich mix of data.

A weakness of usability testing is that "user" is not the same concept as "customer." Where usability testing focuses on use, the concept of customer encompasses of the investigating, buying, installing, and evaluating of products, as well as their use. In business-to-business contexts, the product user may be only one of several distinct constituencies whose needs have to be understood and addressed. In short, a product can attain a high degree of excellence in ease of use and still fail to be customer focused in a broader sense.

A second weakness of usability testing is that it is primarily reactive rather than proactive. What you study is the user's response to a prototype that you designed. This weakness becomes less serious when usability testing is used appropriately, later on in a development process, and when usability testing is done iteratively rather than on a one-shot basis. As an aside, in some technology companies, usability specialists have expanded their role to fill a vacuum left by a weak or absent marketing function. In such situations, *usability testing,* defined as any activity in which usability specialists get involved, typically expands to include other market research techniques, such as customer visits, focus groups, and survey research. For purposes of clarity, however, I think it is best to give usability testing a narrow definition as above, while acknowledging that a corporate focus on improving usability often will require the involvement of usability specialists in multiple market research techniques in addition to usability testing proper.

Contextual Inquiry

The distinguishing feature of contextual inquiry is that product designers watch customers using a product at the customer's place of work. Contextual inquiry can thus be thought of as a specialized kind of customer visit or as a field approach to usability studies. As part of contextual inquiry, designers discuss with users what they just did or what just happened. The basic idea is that so much of a user's product experience is tacit or taken for granted that it cannot be effectively vocalized or discussed unless the user is placed in context—that is, examined while doing their job. Moreover, in contrast to usability testing, the presumption is that the designers do not necessarily know which tasks are important or very much about the nature of these tasks, hence the need to observe customers in context.

As to procedure, designers first meet to identify areas of interest and uncertainty with respect to product design. This should culminate in a list of activities to observe and events to notice. Customers are then recruited to participate as in any customer visit program. Typically a team of designers will go to a customer site, fan out, and each spend 1 or 2 hours with a user in the user's cubicle as the user performs work using the product of interest. Several such site visits will be made so that a dozen or more observations accumulate. These experiences then become inputs to the remainder of the product definition activities and are analyzed similarly to any qualitative study.

The specific technique just described emerged at Digital Equipment in the 1980s. It is ideal for topics such as design of the visual interface of a product, in which the user is unlikely to be able to retrieve and discuss failures and shortcomings unless actually engaged in the use of the interface. Contextual inquiry also shares in the strength of any observational technique: It gets beyond the customer's self-report. Furthermore, as with any field research technique, it also takes designers out of the laboratory and places them in the customer's world.

The key weakness can be highlighted as follows: How would you react if someone watched you work *and* interrupted you with questions as they saw fit? How much work would you get done, and how representative of your actual work experience would this vignette be? Rather than approached as a total solution, contextual inquiry might be thought of as one of many good things that can be done during a customer visit and as something that you ought to at least try if you have not yet done so.

The real value of contextual inquiry in my mind is that it raises the questions of what form an *anthropological* approach to customer research might take. By contrast, most customer research historically has been psychological, social psychological, or sociological in inspiration. Controlled experiments, usability testing, and conjoint analysis build on the idea of a psychological laboratory as pioneered in Germany a century ago. Customer visits, focus groups, and some survey research build on social psychological concepts developed in the early decades of this century. Survey research, in general, and much secondary research build on sociological ideas dating back many years. By contrast, the distinctive methodology of anthropology has been ethnographic study and participant observation. Specifically, anthropologists perform their studies by going to live with the natives in their village. They converse, they observe, *and* they participate in the life of the village. None of the traditional techniques of market research quite correspond to this anthropological model.

From this perspective, contextual inquiry is only the tip of the iceberg. Some consumer packaged goods companies have felt the need to go beyond customer interviews to on-site observation of, say, how laundry detergent or dishwater soap actually is used in the household. Similarly, some manufacturers of industrial goods have sent representatives to spend a week watching their product in use at the customer's factory. The videocamera offers a key technological support for this kind of study, being both thorough and unobtrusive in its observation. The benefits of the physical immersion in the life of the customer that a weeklong visit permits, however, are not to be underestimated. The anthropological approach is distinguished, then, by the intensity of its engagement with a small number of customers. Adaptations of the basic anthropological approach can be expected to proliferate as vendors seek to get ever closer to customers and to more thoroughly instill the customer perspective in key employees. Contextual inquiry is one example of how to proceed.

Computer Simulations

Computer simulations share the goal of any laboratory technique: to reproduce under controlled conditions a faithful replica of some real-world circumstance of interest. Today this is done with high-quality video monitors running multimedia software: In the not-too-distant future, virtual reality techniques will provide even more faithful replicas. The following two examples will clarify the potential.

EXAMPLE 1

Ray Burke at Harvard has developed a computerized interactive approach to the test of package designs. A large video monitor shows an image of a supermarket shelf. One's own package or any new package design can be placed on the shelf in the midst of competitor's packages exactly as it would appear in a real store. Participants in the study can navigate the aisle by means of a mouse. If they desire to examine a package more closely (as we all do from time to time while shopping), consumers can zoom in on the package and display ingredients, fat content, or anything else that might be printed on a package. Best of all, the software tracks and measures everything the participant does. Consequently, one can run experiments using different package designs and measure their effectiveness in various ways.

EXAMPLE 2

Researchers at Massachusetts Institute of Technology (MIT) have experimented with a technique they call information acceleration as a way of doing market research on very new products. A computerized system allows participants to see, examine, and search for information on a new product concept. The goal is to go beyond a simple description ("This electric car has a range of 100 miles." "It can be charged from any household outlet . . .") to replicate the actual information search process that consumers would go through when contemplating purchase of a new product. The computer system can provide, when requested by consumers participating in the study, simulated product reviews, word-of-mouth testimony, comparative performance ratings, or any other information that consumers might employ in deciding whether to adopt an innovation. By replicating the search process rather than simply providing a passive description, the approach hopes to make the new product concept sufficiently vivid and give it enough presence that consumers can render meaningful judgments as to its attractiveness or drawbacks, thus helping the manufacturer to evaluate the potential of the new product and diagnose strengths and weaknesses. Absent such an in-depth approach, the fear always has been that consumer reactions to very new products are relatively useless because consumers have no clear idea of the product that they are asked to evaluate.

Any computerized simulation enjoys several advantages. First, one can readily create experimental conditions and easily measure a variety of effects simply by altering the controlling software so it presents different images or alternatives. Moreover, because stimulus presentation is computerized, the experiment is executed consistently for each participant. Finally, a computer using multimedia software permits a much more faithful replica of real-world conditions, thus enhancing the realism of the experiment and increasing the probability that the same results will be obtained outside the laboratory.

Summary

Yet other new techniques in market research can be expected to extend each of the two quite distinct directions illustrated by the examples in this chapter. Along one front, innovation will follow the track laid down by choice modeling and experimentation. These new techniques will make use of ever more sophisticated mathematical models and ever more intensive laboratory constructions, as seen in the computer simulation examples. Along the other front, following the track laid down by focus groups and customer visits, vendors will seek ever more intimate engagement with the real world of their customers, as seen in the example of contextual inquiry. Finally, some techniques will unite high tech and high touch, the experimental and the anthropological poles, as seen in some kinds of usability testing. The days when *market research* basically meant *survey research* are long past.

Suggested Reading

Holtzblatt, K., & Beyer, H. (1993). Making customer-centered design work for teams. *Communications of the ACM, 36,* 93-103.

>This article provides a discussion of the contextual inquiry method by one of its founders.

Klemmer, E. T. (1989). *Ergonomics: Harness the power of human factors in your business.* Norwood, NJ: Ablex.

Nielsen, J. (1993). *Usability engineering.* New York: Academic Press.

Norman, D. A. (1990). *The design of everyday things.* New York: Doubleday.

>Although the entire field of usability testing is still being invented, these works will provide an entry point. Plan on searching trade journals and conference proceedings in the computer and software engineering areas for the most up-to-date material.

In addition, the American Marketing Association sponsors an annual conference on advanced research techniques, which provides an opportunity to learn about new and emerging techniques.

10

Combining Research Techniques Into Strategies

It is rarely the case that a business problem can be addressed by the application of a single research technique in isolation. More commonly, multiple complementary research techniques, conducted in sequence, are required. This chapter describes the kind of complete research strategy that might be developed to address five common business problems. The examples given are "pure" cases, showing what you might do when the magnitude of the problem justifies it and your budget permits. In actual cases, one or more of the techniques described might be omitted, for the very good reason that the payback for the research expenditure would be too small, in accordance with the calculations described in Chapter 1. Other combinations of techniques also could be used; these sequences are intended to be illustrative and not rigid prescriptions.

Developing New Products

■ Use secondary research to assess existing product offerings from competitors and to estimate market size and growth rates in this category. Secondary data also can be used to build a financial justification for any proposed product.

■ Conduct customer visits among potential buyers for the new product. These visits will identify unmet needs and areas of dissatisfaction with existing offerings. Participation in the visits by engineering staff will assist them throughout the project in visualizing how customers might respond to various design trade-offs.

■ Execute a choice modeling study to identify the optimal combination of features and functionality from among several design alternatives produced in response to the secondary research and customer visits.

■ Do a usability test to ensure that the product as designed works as intended.

■ Conduct an experiment to estimate profitability and market share for the new product at each of several prices.

Assessing Customer Satisfaction

■ Use secondary research to find any public information on competitors' level of customer satisfaction in addition to any data on one's own level of customer satisfaction that outsiders might have gathered. In addition to this quantitative data, search the literature for more qualitative data: What are key dissatisfiers or common complaints? What are crucial needs that must be addressed by any satisfactory solution? Analyze your own internal records to identify themes running through complaints and calls to the service department, for example.

■ Conduct customer visits to identify and explore how customers evaluate their satisfaction with this product category, what standards they use to assess product quality, and how intangibles such as vendor reputation come into play. The goal here is to learn *what* to measure.

■ Conduct a survey of customers at regular intervals to numerically measure and track customer satisfaction. This survey needs to draw a representative sample, and it needs to be executed consistently over time. Precisely and accurately measure the factors you earlier identified and explored via secondary research and customer visits.

■ Follow up on surprising, unexpected, or confusing results with a program of customer visits. Although surveys will tell you *that* something is wrong, they will not always explain *why* customers are less satisfied or what improvements need to be done.

Segmenting a Market

■ Use secondary research to identify possible segmentation schemes proposed by industry analysts or actually in use by competitors. Pay close attention to internal secondary data in the form of sales records and customer databases. Exploratory analyses of this internal data may suggest significant differences among existing customers.

■ Use focus groups to explore psychological differences among customers. These might concern values or benefits desired or intangible cultural or lifestyle differences. Focus groups are helpful in this application because participants often polarize around discussion of certain issues, thus highlighting possible segment differences. The goal is to discover new ways to segment the market.

■ Conduct customer visits to explore in depth the characteristics of the possible segments identified through secondary research and focus groups. The visits will assist in developing a detailed profile of each segment and also may suggest new segments or new ways to reconfigure the tentative segmentation scheme.

■ Conduct a survey to accurately measure the size and characteristics of each segment in the tentative scheme. Although your earlier research has generated possible segments, it cannot confirm that any particular segment is large enough to be worthwhile or whether the tentative segments actually differ in the marketplace to the degree suggested by your research studies. Because segmentation analyses are typically a prelude to a decision to target one or a small number of segments, it is important to do survey research to accurately assess how attractive each individual segment might be.

■ Conduct a choice modeling study to understand how brand perceptions and product preferences differ across segments of interest. Given two or more targeted segments whose attractiveness has been demonstrated through survey research, the question now becomes how to develop differentiated messages and actual products that precisely address the distinctive wants and needs of each targeted segment. The choice modeling study can show how perceptions of your brand differ across segments, providing a focus for future advertising efforts and showing how importance weights differ, directing product development efforts.

Expanding Into New Markets

Here, the notion is that you might be able to sell current or modified products to new types of customers.

■ Use secondary research to identify attractive markets not currently served. A comparison of industry data to your own sales records and customer databases will help to identify underserved or neglected markets. Profiles of competitors might reveal to you unsuspected market niches or areas where, despite good sales volume, you have barely penetrated.

■ Conduct focus groups to gain initial insights into the thought world and point of view of members of untapped markets. Focus groups tend to be a time-efficient means of grasping the basic outline of an unfamiliar worldview.

■ Conduct customer visits to more thoroughly describe applications, usage environments, and organizational decision processes of these untapped markets. The observational component and the in-depth nature of the interaction makes visits a useful supplement to focus groups.

■ Conduct a survey to more thoroughly describe the size characteristics and potential of the one or more new markets under study. (Note that the same logic applies to markets as to segments within markets.)

■ Conduct a choice modeling study to grasp what is important and unimportant to these people so as to develop or select the best product configuration with which to attack this new market.

Developing an Advertising Campaign

■ Use secondary research to identify competitors' level of spending, relative emphasis on various media, and choice of particular vehicles. Gather, as well, examples of competitors' actual ads so as to identify themes and appeals.

■ Conduct focus groups to gain insight into customers' thinking and to understand the kinds of issues that are important and unimportant to them. It will be important to have both vendor marketing staff and advertising agency personnel be involved with these focus groups.

■ Conduct a survey to describe brand image of self and competitors, current levels of awareness, and specific beliefs or perceptions about your brand. The goal here is partly to verify findings from the focus groups and partly to measure baseline levels of factors, such as awareness, that the advertising campaign is supposed to influence.

■ Conduct an experiment to compare the relative effectiveness of several alternative executions, each of which is on strategy, in the sense of addressing issues uncovered in the earlier research, but each of which takes a somewhat different creative approach. Sometimes the goal here will be to pick the strongest execution and at other times it will be to rank order the effectiveness of a larger group so that the more effective executions receive a larger share of the media budget.

■ Conduct a survey to track the effectiveness of the campaign. This survey will repeat measurements made during the baseline survey.

Commentary

The common theme across most of these research strategies should be apparent: The canonical sequence of techniques in devising a research strategy is first, secondary research; second, customer visits or focus groups for exploratory purposes; and third, surveys, choice modeling, and experiments for confirmatory purposes. Again, your specific application may differ so that other sequences or more extended sequences also may be valid. Moreover, much depends on the unique circumstances of your case as to whether a particular technique needs to be executed at all. But the canonical sequence, stated more generally, serves as a useful summary for the marketing research advice given in this book:

First, look around.
Second, explore deeply.
Third, make sure.
Fourth, measure results.

Index

147

About the Author

Edward F. McQuarrie is Associate Professor in the Department of Marketing at Santa Clara University. He received his Ph.D. in Social Psychology from the University of Cincinnati in 1985. His research interests include implementation of a market focus, qualitative research, and technology strategy. His book, *Customer Visits: Building a Better Market Focus,* was published in 1993 by Sage. He has published articles in the *Journal of Consumer Research, Journal of Product Innovation Management, Marketing Research, Journal of the Market Research Society, Computers in Human Behavior,* and *Social Science Computer Review* and has reviewed books on focus groups and qualitative research for the *Journal of Marketing Research.* He has received grants from the National Endowment for the Humanities, the National Science Foundation, and the Marketing Science Institute.

Dr. McQuarrie has 12 years of experience moderating focus groups for Burke Marketing Research of Cincinnati. He has consulted for a variety of technology firms and has taught seminars on effective customer visits, managing focus group research, and similar topics for Hewlett-Packard, Sun Microsystems, Apple Computer, Compaq, Fluke, Motorola, Varian Associates, CIGNA, Cadence Design, and other clients.